The KEY to winning is as simple as ABC

Accelerated Bible Concept

Losing is not an option when you are playing for keeps.

HEAVEN RULES

FAYE ALDRIDGE

DAVIS JACKSON PUBLISHERS
LEBANON, TN 37087
www.DavisJacksonPublishers.com

ISBN 0988742802

Manuscript written by Faye Aldridge
Designer: Alison Griffin, www.amGriffinDesign.com
Author Photo: Jacob Layne

Dedication

As a token of my appreciation

I dedicate this book to our

Heavenly Father

for all of His marvelous gifts.

Acknowledgment

A special thanks to my dear friend,

Peggy Culbert, who saw great potential

in this little book from the very

beginning. She offered

an honest opinion, daily

encouragement, persistent prayers

and her beneficial editing skills.

I offer you my sincere thanks, Peggy!

Contents

1 | A WEDDING 9

2 | FAVOR 19

3 | THE KEY...25

4 | ABC..31

5 | SATURATION 43

6 | DOCUMENTED CASES OF ABC RESULTS...51

7 | A CHANGE OF HEART.................................63

8 | WHEN WE REPENT 73

9 | LOVE NEVER FAILS 81

10 | FAITH DEFIES LOGIC 91

11 | WE HAVE HOPE 101

12 | BLUE SKY..111

13 | HEAVEN..121

14 | HELL..129

15 | DISCERNMENT 139

CONCLUSION..150

the KEY

The **Bible**

is a supernatural **Key**

and it unlocks the door

leading us to where **God**

wants us to be.

ABC

Accelerated Bible Concept

is a specific method by which anyone can tap into the power of the Bible in an unprecedented manner. Completion of the ABC process requires less than 90 days. The Bible is the KEY. In past experiences, I discovered that **reading the Bible in a compressed time period** produced astonishing results and life changes! The outcome affected me spiritually, emotionally and circumstantially. Anyone willing to follow my example, as described in this book, can benefit greatly from accessing the **Key by ABC**.

1

*A marriage…makes of two fractional lives
a whole; it gives to two purposeless lives a work
and doubles the strength of each to perform
it. It gives to two questioning natures a reason
for living and something to live for. It gives
a new gladness to sunshine, a new fragrance
to the flowers, a new beauty to the earth
and a new mystery to life!¹ ~ Mark Twain*

1

A Wedding

On June 20, 1969, there was a wedding at Mt. Vernon Baptist Church in a small southern town. It was a small, sweet, country style wedding. The little church sat at the edge of a wooded area accessible by way of a gravel road. Gardenia blossoms filled the sanctuary and their sweet fragrance wafted through the air on that hot summer evening. The aged piano never sounded better as the traditional wedding song resonated through the quaint little chapel. A smiling young bride wearing a simple satin and lace gown walked slowly down the aisle, joining the groom at the front of the church. The bride and groom said their vows and the preacher pronounced them husband and wife, reminding them the marriage vows were valid until death separated them.

The young ages of the bride and groom were to their disadvantage. Immaturity and unrealistic expectations led them to divorce only three months later. The girl went home to live with her mother. Gossips spread the news and many claimed it was all a mistake, a marriage that never had a chance of working in the first place.

The newly decreed divorcee was a seamstress and she went to work each day pretending things were fine. She did not want to admit it but she was very unhappy. Sometimes, she prayed but she knew little about the power of prayer, faith and God except for the fact that God was up there somewhere. Still, she made an attempt and she prayed she could *'go back in time and start all over again'*. She wondered if miracles really happened.

Weeks and months came and went, leaving her feeling like the lone occupant of a little rowboat in the middle of the ocean with no land in sight. Confused and disappointed, she knew of no remedy for her situation. The young woman felt sad and to make matters worse, she missed her ex-husband. She realized she still cared for him.

There was no sense crying over unfortunate circumstances. The couple parted on very unfriendly terms and there was a double portion of animosity between them. Neither of them had been willing to give an inch or ask forgiveness for angry words spoken in haste. She had no way of knowing where he was or what he was doing. The man and woman equally shared the blame for their divorce and it was finished; *or was it?*

In mid February, the woman felt compelled to search for the Bible she received at the age of ten. At that young age, she had attended a revival, accepted Jesus as her Savior and received Baptism. The woman's Bible was located in a dresser drawer. As soon as she put her hand on it, she began reading on the very first page in the book of Genesis. "In the beginning God created the heavens and the earth, and the earth was formless and void, and darkness was over the surface of the deep; and the Spirit of God was moving over the surface of the waters." She read until her eyelids grew heavy and sleep overtook her.

The Bible contained various names the woman could not pronounce correctly and she did not understand all she read but that did not stop her. Each evening after work, she opened the Bible and she read every word on every line on every page and strangely, the words comforted her. How could she have known the Bible is a living force and it is Holy, powerful and life changing? The Word is the Mind of God.

> For the Word of God is living and active and sharper than any two-edged sword, and piercing as far as

the division of soul and spirit, of both joints and marrow and able to judge the thoughts and intentions of the heart. *Hebrews 4:12*

Less than 90 days from the time she began reading on the first page, she reached the end, the book of Revelation. In the first chapter of the last book of the Bible, she read the words, "Blessed is he who reads and those who hear the words of the prophecy and heed the things which are written in it." She was surprised when she read that Scripture and learned that a blessing is promised to anyone who simply reads the Bible!

By now, you may be wondering how I know so much about the woman. *I was that young bride and even now, I still have an excellent memory.*

One evening after work, I entered my bedroom to put some things in the closet. Suddenly, I heard a voice speak two words to me. Those two words were spoken deliberately, forcefully and without repetition. I heard, "Go now". I did not think it strange that I heard a holy voice speaking to me. I did not hesitate to obey the voice. I neither rushed nor tarried. There was no anxiety in me as I gathered my car keys and purse and unquestioningly walked out of the house into the darkness to get in my car.

I began my drive on a dark, country road with a certain unspoken knowledge that I should drive in a northern direction although I was uncertain of my destination. I drove along in perfect peace as if I had an internal navigation system directing me. I ended up more than twenty miles and two small towns away from where I started. As I drove on a narrow asphalt road, the light beams from my headlights landed briefly on a man walking toward me.

I had no sooner passed him than I realized the man was Burke, my ex-husband. I turned the car around and drove back, pulling over onto the shoulder of the road to see if I could drive him somewhere. Pointing in the direction of his destination, Burke assured me he was walking only the shortest distance to a small country store near the home in which he was staying. The engine on his motorcycle had failed to start, forcing him to walk. He slid onto the car seat beside me.

Miraculously, all the unpleasant memories vanished. We were both genuinely glad to see each other. We tried to speak at the same time! I felt no surprise; instead, I felt like our meeting was planned. We laughed and talked as dear friends do when they are enjoying a pleasant encounter. We drove to a café in a nearby town and talked late into the evening. Everything that transpired that night felt perfectly normal. Less than a week later, my husband and I remarried.

We lived a good life together, far from perfect, but overall, a good and happy life. God blessed us with two healthy children; we had a lovely daughter and a wonderful son. Later on, we had three beautiful grandchildren! Our family was loving and closely knit. We led productive lives, worked, built a beautiful home, traveled and enjoyed a lifetime that might have been enviable to some who were not as fortunate. There were difficult times but we always managed to work through them. Our marriage lasted 35 years until Burke died in 2005. In hindsight, I took a lot for granted, never considering precisely how all those happy years really came to be.

In 2011, the Lord began to shine His perfect and revealing light on that miraculous unexpected meeting with Burke so long ago. I suppose He wanted me to acknowledge His gift so I could give Him thanks, even though belated. By early 2012, I had a new attitude of gratitude and a new comprehension of that particular gift. The gift was His answer to the prayer I prayed at the age of seventeen, in 1970. God gave me precisely what I asked for, the chance to go back and start all over again. I was astounded that it took me so long to comprehend the significance of His miraculous gift. The gift materialized after a series of events were set into motion by Divine intervention. That miraculous gift was an answer to my prayer and it affected others and me for a lifetime.

God caused me to see that our lives from 1970 through 2005 began with two simple little words. In my mind, I traveled back in time pouring over the details of the past, recalling that night I heard the voice instructing me to, "Go now". I remembered the night Burke and I came face to face, seemingly by coincidence.

- First, there was the motor cycle engine failure that necessitated walking instead of riding.

- The short distance Burke had to walk that evening took only five minutes. If I had been three minutes earlier or three minutes later, we would have missed each other completely. Our reunion that night would not have happened.

- There was only one little window of time in which

our paths could have crossed that night.

- There was no room for the slightest error. Perfect timing was essential.

- Divine intervention operated in precision on our behalf.

- Discernment was necessary and obedience was crucial for a successful outcome according to Heaven Rules.

- God orchestrated our circumstances! Angelic watchers from the Heavenly realm worked in harmony; silently, invisibly and successfully carrying out their mission!

If God had sounded an alarm in advance, surely Satan would have caused a distraction to thwart the opportunity that night. We must never forget that Satan is real and he wants to 'steal, kill and destroy' (John 10:10) what God strongly desires to give us. God sometimes carries out His plans as 'shrewdly as a serpent, as innocently as a dove', (Matthew 10:16) working covertly, with speed, precision and accuracy to accomplish matters before Satan knows what is going on. When we pray for an answer, we must be able to hear His voice and be willing to respond in obedience in order to receive the answer.

It seems like many prayers go unanswered, however; consider how many times GOD has orchestrated a plan to answer us, and then spoken…and we failed to hear Him.

2

Joseph found God's favor, as told in Genesis 39:21. After a time of struggle and adversity, God gave Joseph financial abundance and the highest rank in the land, second only to Pharaoh. God granted Moses favor and honor then used him as a chosen vessel to lead his people out of bondage in the land of Egypt. The Bible tells of many cases where God's favor caused prominence, recognition and promotions. Rules, regulations and laws were changed supernaturally to create favor on Queen Esther's behalf resulting in the preservation of the Jewish people. There were times when God actually fought battles for human beings because they found favor in His eyes. When we strive to find favor in God's eyes, I believe that is pleasing to Him. Seeking God through His Holy Word is one sure way to find His favor. The Bible is the KEY.

Favor

In 1970, at the age of seventeen, it was impossible for me to foresee that God would involve me in a plan requiring a 40 year incubation period before illumination. At that young age, I could not comprehend the magnitude of the answered prayer described in chapter one or the far-reaching effects of the gift of God's favor that I stumbled upon. The answer to that prayer came as a consequence of God's favor. I discovered God's favor when I read the Bible in a compressed time-period.

The answered prayer set in motion circumstances that reshaped my life. That is monumental in itself but astounding now that I realize God caused all that to happen in preparation for this very day, more than 40 years later! The words I have written, the words you are now reading, are not by accident but precisely by design according to God's plan and Heaven Rules.

What is favor? Favor is something that is granted out of goodwill or as a gesture of admiration. It is the state of being regarded and noticed, perhaps by one who is superior. One who favors us might decide to show us excessive kindness or preferential treatment.

God's favor is a true manifestation of God's plan for our lives. It does not come to us because we deserve it. It comes from God's goodness and many times, it comes as a consequence of an action that triggers His response.

> If we trust in the Lord with all our hearts, we know He will make our paths straight. *Proverbs 3:5-6*

> If we search for the Lord with all our hearts, we know we will find Him. *Deuteronomy 4:29*

> Good understanding produces favor. *Proverbs 13:15*

One simple truth I have discovered, in alignment with these Scriptures, is: When I read the entire Bible in less than 90 days, I found favor in God's sight. When I entered God's presence for a prolonged time-period, by reading His Word, He responded by showing His love and approval in the form of His favor. He also brought about an answer to my complex prayer that actually allowed me to go back in time and start all over again, as if time was insignificant. Time is insignificant to God for He is Master of all, even time. Here is an example showing how insignificant time really is to God considering His immeasurable power. This is a documented Biblical account of how God turned back the hands of time, as a sign, when He answered one simple prayer Hezekiah prayed.

- Then Hezekiah turned his face to the wall, and prayed to the Lord, and said, "Remember now, O Lord, I beseech Thee, how I have walked before Thee in truth and with a whole heart, and have done what is good in Thy sight." Hezekiah wept bitterly.

- Then the Word of the Lord came to Isaiah, saying, "Go and say to Hezekiah, 'Thus says the Lord, the God of your father David, I have heard your prayer, I have seen your tears, behold, I will add fifteen years to your life'." This shall be the sign to you from the Lord, that the Lord will do this thing that He has spoken. "Behold, I will cause the shadow on the stairway, which has gone down with the sun on the stairway of Ahaz, to go back ten steps." So the sun's shadow went back ten steps on the stairway on which it had gone down. (Isaiah 38:2-8)

- Hezekiah reminded God of his faithful service to Him. He wanted to 'find favor in God's sight', in his hour of need. He knew that his service had pleased God in the past and he wanted to remind God of his obedient walk to move Him to answer his prayer for a miracle. Hezekiah needed God to grant him the gift of His favor. God granted Hezekiah's request and granted him an additional 15 years of life. God caused time to move backward, and the hands of time reversed, simply to prove His point to Hezekiah!

- I keep this one particular fact in mind at all times. God can do anything!

We cannot imagine all the Father will do for us if we believe He is able, and He is surely able to do all things, for He is Almighty God! What resource could ever be as valuable as finding favor in the sight of God? Reading the Bible in a compressed time-period is one pathway to the place of His favor. I found His favor and it created amazing life changes for me.

If that course of action worked successfully for me, surely it will work successfully for all who want to follow my example! God's Word is very powerful and it becomes even more powerful and prolific when one reads the entire Bible in a compressed time-period. God's Word is powerful enough to affect hearts, minds and circumstances for individuals, families, students, churches, work forces and nations!

We are living in a time when the world seems to be spiraling out of control and away from God. We desperately need to hear from God regarding the challenging times we face! It is not by coincidence that God has revealed this simple yet powerful gift, consisting of the Key, ABC and His favor in the year of 2012. The gift is yours if you choose to make it yours! If you have a desire to discover what God has in store for you, you must make a choice and a decision, then act on that decision, taking hold of the Key by ABC!

I hope you will come along with me as I explain details about the KEY, ABC, God's favor and some Heaven Rules throughout the unfolding pages of this book!

3

*There is a small disc on the Meades Ranch
in north central Kansas where the thirty-
ninth parallel from the Atlantic to the Pacific
crosses the ninety-eighth meridian running
from Canada to the Rio Grande. The National
Oceanic Survey, a small federal agency whose
business it is to locate the exact positions
of every point in the United States, uses the
scientifically recognized reference point on the
Meades Ranch. So far, no mistakes have been
made and none are expected.*

*All ocean-liners and commercial planes come
under the survey. The government can build
no dams or even launch a missile without this
agency to tell it the exact location to the very
inch. "Location by approximation can be costly
and dangerous." If the 'point of reference' from
which the surveyor takes his measurements is
wrong, all of his calculations will be wrong.
Where you start determines where you end.[2] The
Bible is our reference point.*

2

The Key

In recent years, my Heavenly Father revealed to me that it was the deliberate act and completion of reading the Bible in less than 90 days that led me to the place where I first encountered His favor. He also allowed me to comprehend the BIBLE is the KEY that unlocks the door between Heaven and earth. The Bible is alive and it is supernatural, meaning it derives its' power from God and it cannot be explained in logical terms or understood fully by the human mind. We have to comprehend it by allowing the Holy Spirit to interpret, translate and impart the words to us, in terms we can understand.

The Bible is our reference point. It is like a compass, and if we make our choices and decisions based on the accuracy of the Bible, the Lord will make our paths straight. The Bible provides direction for our everyday lives and our spiritual journeys and helps us navigate the roads of life.

The Bible is from God. God spoke the words through the Holy Spirit and the Prophets recorded the words.

The Bible is truth. It shines holy light into the darkness. It tells the truth about God and redemption through Jesus Christ.

The Bible is a surrogate or a replacement for many resources that may not be available to us due to insufficient finances or unsatisfactory circumstances. For example, when acquiring a college education is not possible, the Bible is able to fill the void created by a lack of advanced education. A strong faith in God can lead us to wonderful opportunities and situations God has placed in our paths. Theodore Roosevelt, the 26th President of the United States once said, "A thorough understanding of the Bible is better than a college education." How completely right he was in his assumption and President Roosevelt spoke after having reached the highest office in the land.

The Bible fills our hearts and minds with strong faith, powerful enough to summon food in famines, healing in the absence of modern medicine and protection in the face of certain death.

In First Kings 17:4, we learn interesting facts about Elijah by the brook Cherith, which is east of the Jordan River. The Lord told him to drink from the brook, then said to him, "I have commanded the ravens to provide for you there." For more than three years, the ravens flew to Elijah twice daily, bringing him food.

I heard of a poor family that faced a fierce winter one year. The small amount of food they had never lasted as long as they wished it would. A couple of days each week, the family went hungry. One day, they were extremely hungry and they saw no solution. Suddenly, a large flock of birds swooped in and landed very near the front of the house. Those birds became a delicious meal later that evening. The Lord provided!

The Bible yields an abundance of resources that we need to live our lives, like faith, hope and love. Faith comes by hearing and hearing by the Word of Christ. (Romans 10:8). It gives us direction, peace, strength, comfort, wisdom, understanding, knowledge and healing. The Bible is so powerful that it can redirect our lives to exact locations the Lord chooses for us. If we had to purchase what the Bible provides for us, we could never earn the money to obtain it, for the Bible is priceless. It is a holy document containing God's laws and Heaven Rules.

Having some prior knowledge of how God provides for His people may be the reason I was not surprised when He began to reveal certain truths to my mind. God spoke one simple statement into my spirit as the revelation began about the KEY and ABC. He said, "The Bible is a miraculous and supernatural KEY and it unlocks the door leading us to where God wants us to be." The Bible is a living force and it is a KEY, so powerful it can convict our hearts of sin, leading the lost to perfect Salvation through Jesus Christ. I had never thought of the Bible as a key but it made perfect sense! The Bible is a KEY that unlocks the door between Heaven and earth. It is the key to our hearts, our happiness, our resources and our future.

The Bible literally opened a door for me the first time I used the ABC process. In the next chapters, you will see the results of that experience and evidence of God's presence in my life over a period of many years. I dare not think how I would have fared and where I would have ended up without the Lord and His Divine guidance.

4

ABC-Accelerated Bible Concept, is the term I use to describe the method of reading the entire Bible in a compressed period of time. In less than 90 days, a participant can easily complete the ABC process. It is a deliberate act and I believe it pleases our Heavenly Father very much! The accomplishment of this deliberate act is an honorable deed. The deliberate act triggers a specific response. Soon after the completion of accessing the KEY by ABC, expect positive developments to manifest in your spirit, emotions and circumstances.

ABC

Because of a great need, at the age of seventeen, I sought the Lord through His Holy Word, the Bible, as I described in the first chapter. I discovered that when I read the Bible in its entirety in a compressed time-period, (in less than 90 days); God's Holy Word affected me spiritually, emotionally and circumstantially.

In my particular experience, reading the Bible in its entirety meant reading from Genesis to Revelation. I began on page 1 and read each subsequent page thereafter, not skipping pages or chapters. I did not alternate between the Old Testament and the New Testament. I read from the first page to the last in numerical page sequence. I firmly believe there is a powerful significance in adhering strictly to these two requirements.

- Reading the Bible in numerical page sequence (from first page to last page).

- Reading the Bible in less than 90 days.

These are the two important dynamics in achieving a successful outcome in the ABC process. Some may read the Bible in 30 or 60 days and that is acceptable and commendable. The ABC process must be completed in less than 90 days if it is to work successfully.

This deliberate action resulted in a powerful supernatural manifestation that created changes in my life. The completion of the ABC-Accelerated Bible Concept process led me to a place in the spirit that I refer to as a place of God's favor.

My being in that place, set in motion circumstances and happenings in the spirit world that benefited me greatly in the natural world.

- Prayers that remained unanswered before were answered, soon after the completion of the ABC-Accelerated Bible Concept process.

- My prayers were answered in such ways as to defy logic. The answers came by supernatural means and undeniable Divine intervention.

- The prayer the Lord answered in 1970 changed the course of my life, permanently.

- When I reached the end of the Bible in that compressed period of time, I assume, it pleased God, for that was when and where I first found His favor.

In 2011 and 2012, the Lord prompted me over a period of many months, guiding me to a point of understanding. The Holy Spirit gently encouraged me to delve into memories from the past and I did. God allowed me to see each memory through His eyes and with the wisdom of His perfect understanding.

Soon after the Lord imparted to me the knowledge that the 'Bible was a supernatural Key', He also imparted to me the term and the value of the Accelerated Bible Concept-ABC. In His wisdom, He allowed me to see the significance of the amazing 1970 experience and discovery! He reminded me of more recent experiences in 1991 and 2004 which substantiated the authenticity of the amazing 1970 experience. The 2012 experience substantiated the authenticity of the earlier experiences.

God planted a strong desire in me to share His KEY/ABC gift with those individuals who are in need, those who are troubled or searching for answers and solutions to life's problems this very day. God prepared me for a period of 40 years, getting me ready to comprehend, receive and share the 2012 revelation with others.

I have learned that God confirms a matter in which He is involved by using two witnesses. When two witnesses have confirmed a matter, I believe the matter should be shared publicly in an effort to glorify God and to bless His children. That is the reason I decided to write about the KEY and Accelerated Bible Concept - ABC.

- I first experienced ABC in 1970 by reading the Bible, from "first page to last page" in less than 90 days.

- God revealed the ABC and the KEY significance to me during the last months of 2011 and in the first months of 2012.

- I wondered if anyone else had ever reached the same conclusion I did. In 2012, I researched the matter. That was when I learned that a man named Ted Cooper, Jr. discovered a similar principle in 1999.

- Ted read the Bible in exactly 90 days and the experience affected him profoundly. He went through a conversion experience and the experience transformed him from an Agnostic to a Christian.[3]

According to Ted, thousands of people already followed his lead, by way of his ministry. He has written

3

books to facilitate his method of reading the Bible by a process of blending Old and New Testament daily readings.

A statement on Ted's website confirmed a principle I found to be true. Here is what Ted said. "A transformation occurs when one reads the Bible in its entirety in a compressed timeframe."[4] I wholeheartedly agree. Two people discovering principles so similar yet independently of each other and years apart, was indeed a remarkable discovery.

> For as the rain and the snow come down from Heaven, and do not return there without watering the earth, and making it bear and sprout, and furnishing seed to the sower and bread to the eater; so shall My Word be which goes forth from My mouth, it shall not return to Me empty, without accomplishing what I desire and without succeeding in the matter for which I sent it. *Isaiah 55: 10, 11*

I believe your particular level of spiritual development prior to ABC, your unique prayer requests, personal

4

needs and individual desires of the heart may very well influence your total ABC outcome. Remember, our prayers must be in alignment with God's will and not contrary to His holiness and His perfect will. Your results will be whatever God wants to achieve in your life. You may not be able to fully recognize the changes and the ultimate outcome of the changes immediately.

I did not comprehend my outcome for 40 years! However, my lack of comprehension did not cancel the beneficial circumstances that happened as a result of my accessing the KEY by ABC. Hindsight is always 20/20 vision.

I hope you get excited when you begin the ABC! You will grow as you go in His Word! No two people will be affected the same way but I believe it is impossible to read the Bible from front to back in less than 90 days and not be affected in a major way.

The average Bible has 1200 pages. If that is the number of pages in your Bible, and you read 12 to 15 pages a day, you can accomplish your goal. The number of pages in Bibles varies greatly, so you should take the simple step of dividing the total number of pages in your Bible by 90 = the minimum number of pages to be read daily. The act of completion places you in a unique place, spiritually, emotionally and circumstantially.

Few people are courageous enough to begin the Accelerated Bible Concept process and even fewer people are tenacious enough to finish the ABC process because it is a challenge. However, with inspiration and diligence, with your eyes focused on the prize, you can do this.

Successful completion of accessing the KEY by ABC process speaks well for the victorious participant and signals:

- You are willing to let the Lord lead you.

- You are interested in God's plan for you.

- You are truly seeking your purpose in life.

Utilizing the ABC requires work and self-discipline. Those who finish will be affected and it is unlikely that they will ever be the same again! I have always believed:

- Each person has a purpose or he or she would not be on planet earth. I also believe:

- God has a plan for every person and the reason

many people never discover their potential is because they do not know how or where to begin.

- There is no such thing as coincidence or luck. You are now reading this book for a reason, because of Divine intervention.

- The completion of accessing the KEY by ABC process means you have taken the first step in the right direction!

Here are some encouraging true facts to keep in mind as we progress through the following pages.

- The KEY by ABC redirected my whole life in 1970.

- The KEY by ABC caused remarkable happenings to unfold in my life in 1991, 2004 and 2012, as I will explain.

- Reading the Bible in its entirety in 90 days led Ted Cooper, Jr. to Salvation in 1999 and to his own ministry in 2002.

- ABC does not promise the same life-changing

outcome for each person. ABC leads some to Salvation and others to redirected lives, a higher level of spiritual comprehension or varying levels of positive circumstantial enhancement.

- Be encouraged that reading the Word always provides hope for beneficial changes in perfect alignment with God's will!

For God has not given us a spirit of timidity, but of power and discipline.
Second Timothy 1:7

NOTE: The KEY by ABC method should not be confused with regular Bible study or daily devotional reading. Daily Bible study and prayer time is encouraged on a regular basis. The ABC process is a separate and unique process focused entirely on reading every word and every line in the Bible as rapidly as possible, in a compressed time-period, not to exceed 90 days.

This rapid process does not allow time for study, reflection, total comprehension or even correct pronunciation of all words. This method works wonders because this reading process is done by faith, allowing the Holy Spirit to interpret and translate essential truths for the reader, causing a miraculous and supernatural benefit to occur. If you expect to reach a successful conclusion in accessing the KEY by ABC, you should adhere to the proven method as described earlier. I encourage you to resume your regular Bible study and devotion time at the end of the ABC process.

5

Hermann Von Helmholtz, a nineteenth century physicist, described 'creative thought' as occurring in three stages: (1) saturation, (2) incubation and (3) illumination. A century later and without prior knowledge of Von Helmholtz, theoretical physicist Murray Gell-Mann came up with a similar theory. [5]

'Creativity is a representation of our unique perspective to a situation or problem'. When confronted with a problem, Gell-Mann endeavored to 'fill his mind with the problem', and the difficulties in question. Next, he tried every way he knew to overcome the problem. When he failed and further conscious thought was useless, he continued to carry the problem around with him. Later, when he least expected it, the answer suddenly manifested 'in his mind'. It is significant to recognize the answer

---

5

to the problem came to his mind, however; the answer did not materialize in reality and it did not manifest in his circumstances. His answer was merely a shadow of the actual solution that comes forth as a result of faith.

Interestingly, when I am confronted by a problem, I 'fill my mind with the answer', meaning Scriptures from God's Word. That is saturation. Waiting, praying and trusting God for the desired outcome provides a time of incubation. In God's perfect timing, the solution comes by illumination.

Filling myself with the problem has never helped me but filling myself with God's answers and focusing on the holy outcome by faith has been proven successful. Faith brings about the answer and solution, 'not only inside the mind, but also outwardly'. Faith brings visible changes in life events, revealing the outcome of faith evidenced in things, people and places.

Saturation

The Lord revealed more and more to me with each passing day in 2012, allowing me to understand the significance of all that really happened to me as a direct result of reading the entire Bible in a compressed time-period. It is my nature to question everything and I asked the Lord, "How did the ABC work and why did the ABC work?"

SATURATION was the word He imparted to me repeatedly in reference to the WORD (the Bible). What is the real meaning of the word 'saturation'?

- Saturation is the state or process that occurs when no more of something can be absorbed, combined or added,

- Saturation is holding as much water or moisture as can be absorbed, thoroughly soaked.

In my spirit, the Lord conveyed to me that I was able to HEAR and OBEY Him that night in 1970 when He said, 'Go now', because His Word saturated my heart and spirit. I had absorbed as much WORD as could be absorbed, I was thoroughly soaked and saturated. The deliberate act of reading the Bible in a compressed period of time caused SATURATION. Saturation caused necessary changes within my spirit. The Word supernaturally modified my soul and the healing effects remained as long as I was overflowing with the Word. The spiritual changes made it possible for the Holy Spirit to work in me and for me by God's design for optimum results.

SATURATION placed me in the position to receive God's favor. God brought about the answer to my prayer. The Lord orchestrated the circumstances necessary to bring about completion. The Bible was the KEY and reading the entire Bible in a compressed period of time, according to the Accelerated Bible Concept-ABC, swiftly activated God's power!

I would like to use this analogy to convey my comprehension of how the KEY and saturation in the Word affected the human being and the spirit being on the inside of me. It can work the same way for you. I ask you to paint a picture in your mind as part of an illustration. Just picture your spirit as a ship, an enormous ocean liner. Your ship was designed to sail across the ocean, beyond the distant horizon, reaching faraway lands. Now inspect the hull of your ship closely and you will discover there are 774,746 holes in the hull.[6] (That is the number of words in the Bible.) There is no way the ship will sail in that condition. It is not sea worthy.

Considering all those holes in your ship's hull, what would you do if you found a way to plug every hole, making it airtight and as good as new? Would you do it? Do you want to find what God has prepared for you? There is a way. I suggest that you now read from the Bible, reading the first line in the book of Genesis. "In the beginning God created the heavens and the earth…"

What if each single word you read in the Bible would plug one single hole in the hull of your ship? See your ship's hull as your spirit, knowing that dealings are possible in the spirit world that are not possible in the natural world. Please keep reading… "And the earth was formless and void…" You have just successfully plugged 17 holes in your ship's hull by reading the first 17 words in the Bible. Remember the analogy. Our spiritual being is lacking and in great need until God's WORD saturates us, filling us with His power. If your spiritual vessel is full of holes, like a tea strainer, God

6

cannot use it the way it was designed to be used. Not until it is airtight, filled to capacity, running over and saturated in the Word of God.

By the time you read the last word in the Bible... YOU WILL HAVE PLUGGED the last hole in your vessel, your spirit. Your ship is now sea worthy and ready to venture out into the deep. The words of wisdom, revelation and knowledge that God pours into you will now stay in you since there are no leaks remaining. You are close to finding the starting point for your new spiritual beginning!

Fast forward, nearly three months. You have just finished reading the entire Bible in less than 90 days and you are saturated. ABC is working for you and you are ready for God's Word to influence you profoundly. Finally, you have found your way to the place where you can receive God's favor and He can carry out His plan for you and in you, according to Heaven Rules! Now that you speak His language, you can hear Him and obey Him! Your actions have triggered a response and placed you in a particular advantageous location.

If I walk outside during a thunderstorm, my hair will get windblown and my clothing will get soaked. A thunderstorm produces rain and wind and it will affect me the same way each time I expose myself to that environment.

If I fill up on God's Word by ABC until the Word literally overflows within me, I will be able to recognize God's voice and obey His commands. The obedience that I act on generates a flow of God's power, working through me. The process then works as it was designed to work and the environment around me is naturally the place where God's favor flows like a river!

In the absence of hindrances, God answers our prayers and that is what He desires to do all the time. His power flows like a river! Disobedience removes the believer from the flowing current to the banks of the river. Miracles happen when we are obedient and we stay in the midst of His river of flowing power!

6

I do not believe there is such a thing in the history of God's eternal kingdom as a right prayer, offered in the right spirit, that remains unanswered. ~ Theodore L. Cuyler

Documented Cases
of ABC Results

Through the years, as I have indicated in the previous chapters, there were other times when I successfully completed the Accelerated Bible Concept (ABC) process. In 1991 and 2004, I had no knowledge about the KEY by ABC. I simply decided to read the Bible during the summer months. Then in 2012 after God revealed the KEY by ABC breakthrough to me, I completed it as a deliberate action, as an experiment. I decided to access the KEY by ABC, fully aware that I was involving myself in an experiment, trusting God for the outcome according to Heaven Rules. At that time, I began officially referring to the process as the ABC Challenge! I proceeded, paying particular attention to changes of any kind. Something incredible happened in the sixty-day period immediately after and because of my successful June 17, 2012, ABC Challenge completion! I will share details about each of those experiences in this chapter but first, I want to point out some interesting details to think about.

> The secret things belong to the Lord our God, but the things revealed belong to us and to our sons forever...
> *Deuteronomy 29:29*

The Accelerated Bible Concept (ABC) theory holds true and has been substantiated each time I have repeated the process. God answered so many prayers for me and consequences of the answered prayers became evident whether the ABC process was completed, intentionally or unintentionally.

I cannot explain decisively how the ABC Challenge works; I only know it does work. I find it beneficial to think of it in logical terms by simple comparisons. When thinking of how ABC Challenge works the metal compass and the First Law of Thermodynamics comes to mind.

First example: The metal compass is a simple device that has a needle where at one end is a small magnet. The needle always points north because the compass picks up the force of the strong magnetic field within the earth. Using the compass, we can consistently determine the direction in which north lies and deduce from that the direction in which we wish to proceed.[7]

7

Human beings are inconsistent. Sometimes, we lose our way in the world. Our life-direction pathways are easily distorted and altered resulting in wrong choices, decisions and lifestyles. I believe the ABC Challenge works like the compass, having the ability to direct our paths and reroute us in the proper direction when we are too confused to know which way to go. The magnetic field of the earth is not man controlled but God controlled. It enables the compass to point us in a northern direction each time we seek the true direction. The Bible is like a holy compass, having a supernatural ability to point us in the right direction whenever we read it and live according to God's laws documented in His Holy Word.

> Thy Word is a lamp unto my feet and a
> light to my path. *Psalm 119:105*

Thermodynamics is a branch of physics dealing with the energy and work of a system. Thermodynamics is the study of relationships involving heat, mechanical work and the aspects of energy and the 'transfer of energy'.[8]

8

Second example: The steam locomotive operates using the First Law of Thermodynamics. When heat is generated by burning fuel (wood or coal) in the locomotive's engine, part of the energy goes into increasing the temperature of the engine's water, which boils and generates steam. What is left is used by the expanding steam to do work and propel the train forward. The constant pressure and volume generates a powerful 'internal energy'. The transfer of that energy releases a particular result, an action, a consequence or a motion.

The ABC Challenge, involves a constant pressure of self-discipline, of reading a constant volume (of pages and words) of God's powerful Words, the Bible, which creates a concentration of 'internal energy'. The 'transfer of that energy' releases power and it results in a particular action, a consequence, a motion! I believe the increased spiritual 'internal energy' specifically alters our circumstances in the natural world! I suppose the changes occur as an automatic response to the 'transfer of internal spiritual energy.'

In 1991, after a powerful personal experience of being born again through the Holy Spirit, I read the Bible for the second time in my life in a compressed time-period, unaware of the ABC significance. I did that during the summer months. The results were as powerful as if I had read the Bible in a compressed time-period, intentionally. These are some of the ways the ABC affected me over the course of 21+ years. It changed me, resulting in:

- **Faith** - to believe for miracles; believing God will do anything I ask of Him if my request is in alignment with His will.

- **Hope** - a sure and steadfast belief that God's goodness will prevail on my behalf, always.

- **Love** - the ability to love God deeply and to love others unconditionally.

- **Forgiveness** - the ability to forgive others as God has forgiven me for bad behavior.

- **Fortitude** - a quality of inner strength that is reflected by an unwillingness to give up.

- **Boldness** - in witnessing in all kinds of places to all kinds of people.

- **Affection** - for God's Word.

- **Perseverance** - to endure when confronted by much adversity.

In the summer of 2004, I determined I would read the entire Bible for the third time in a compressed time-period. I did this during the summer months, as a summer project. I was still unaware of the KEY and ABC significance. Looking back, I am quite certain the Holy Spirit prompted me to 'stock up' on the Word, knowing what lay ahead in the coming months. The outcome strengthened me and prepared me for enormous and unprecedented trials. I was strong enough to survive the death of my husband and the grieving process that followed. These are some of the ways in which accessing the KEY by ABC prepared me and strengthened me over the next eight years.

- **Strength** - in dealing with the death of my husband.

- **Endurance** - in the long grieving process.

- **Courage** - to sell my home and relocate to another city.

- **Trust** - to begin a new career for which I was not trained.

- **Ability** - to write several books as an inexperienced writer. I wrote my first book at the age of 56.

In the spring of 2012, for the fourth time, I began reading the Bible in its entirety in a compressed period of time, in a deliberate manner, with full knowledge of the KEY and Accelerated Bible Concept-ABC. I made the decision to do so after God revealed the concept to me. I had a strong desire to participate in the process by design with real expectations of supernatural manifestations following the completion of the ABC Challenge. God did not disappoint me!

This book idea about the KEY and ABC was conceived during my 2012 ABC Challenge. The book, HEAVEN RULES, emerged from my consciousness in the two months following my completion of the ABC Challenge on June 17, 2012. While it is true that I worked very hard writing the book, I could not have written it without God's influence, through His Holy Spirit. I found favor in God's eyes and the book was His reward and His gift to me. I believe it was His gift that came to me because I completed the ABC Challenge. A spiritual reward awaits each person who successfully completes the ABC Challenge!

Writing this book was a rewarding challenge! I prayed for guidance, inspiration and wisdom in preparation of the text. I understood the Lord had assigned the undertaking to me for the benefit of His people who are living in a troubled world of uncertainty. I also understood God ultimately designed the project for His glory.

> "For everyone to whom much is given, of him shall much be required." *Luke 12:48*

People in all places are looking for a reason to get excited and reach out beyond themselves to grasp real hope, change and inspiration! The place of God's favor is where miracles begin! The ABC-Challenge offers incredible hope and a simple strategy that is available to all men, women and children ages 12+! Completing the ABC Challenge miraculously changes who we are. It changes how we think and how we live. It can lead those who are lost to the point of repentance and surrender, therefore changing where they will spend eternity!

I believe completing the ABC Challenge will affect those who are searching for direction. It will affect those who know the Lord and those who do not know the Lord in a mighty way. The ABC Challenge reminds me of a treasure map leading those who follow it to a certain priceless treasure that has remained hidden from them until now!

"The kingdom of Heaven is like a treasure hidden in the field, which a man found and hid, and   from joy over it, he goes and sells all that he has, and buys that field.

Again, the kingdom of Heaven is like a merchant seeking fine pearls, and upon finding one pearl of great value, he went and sold all that he had and bought it." *Matthew 13:44, 45, 46*

A prayer that I pray for a friend may help in one instance of that person's life. However, if I can accurately convey the significance,   the present and eternal benefits that are produced by accessing the KEY and completing the ABC Challenge, then my friend can be empowered to take an active role in his/her own spiritual successes.

There is no limit to how many times a person can engage in the ABC Challenge. There is no limit to what a person can accomplish and gain from accessing the KEY by the ABC Challenge. I might add, the results are not small results and they are not slow in coming. Success is dependent upon whether or not one is willing to commit, stay the course and diligently pursue the KEY by the ABC process to completion.

I once heard a powerful proverb that describes my passion for sharing the KEY and the ABC. In addition, it describes in part the anticipated personal benefits of the ABC Challenge. It goes like this :

"Give a man a fish and you feed him for a day; teach a man to fish and he will feed himself for a lifetime."

7

If the outer level of our spiritual life with God is impaired to the slightest degree, we must put everything else aside until we make it right. Remember that spiritual vision depends on our character—it is 'the pure in heart' who 'see God'.[9] ~ Oswald Chambers

9

A Change of Heart

Many years ago, I came to the clear realization of the true meaning of the self-destructive effects of hedonism, pride and deception. I had not resisted those domineering influences and consequentially, their influence took a toll on my life and me. Our move to Tennessee in 1978 carried us into a different world with higher earnings and financial opportunities. That was when I restructured my priorities according to my own ideas and ultimately lost my way. I fell away from God. It shocked me and frightened me when I considered what might have happened if God's hand of providence had not moved on my behalf to bring me back into His will and into alignment with Heaven Rules.

You see, I was saved in 1962 and I was saved in 1991. This true statement is sobering. If I was saved in 1962 and I was saved again in 1991 then it becomes apparent that I was lost somewhere in between those two significant dates. So, am I saying Salvation is conditional, that we can lose it if we gradually and insidiously choose to reject and walk away from that precious gift? That is exactly what I am saying. In a moment, I will offer Bible proof, Divine Laws that speak the truth about this absolute reality.

It all began when I accepted Jesus at the age of ten in a small Baptist Church in Goodman, Mississippi at a revival service. I received baptism as a young, innocent child and I was told that I was "saved." In the years that followed my decision at the age of ten, I wrongfully decided that life was not about pleasing God but about pleasing me. I thought life was all about survival, acquiring material possessions, traveling and enjoying the pleasures that money could buy.

Half of my decision to become self-seeking came from growing up in extreme poverty. The other half of my decision came when I allowed myself to be deceived. I allowed my natural human inclinations to prevail without resistance, resulting in pride and hedonism. Pride and hedonism consist of the pursuit of pleasure, a certain arrogance, haughtiness, vanity and conceited self-centeredness. Our society and Satan condone and encourage pride and hedonism. That is deception. Pride and hedonistic attitudes are deceptive distractions that lead us away from God, toward sin and self-destruction.

The boastful 'pride of life', is not from the Father, but is from the world. And the world is passing away, and also its lusts, but the one who does the will of God abides forever. *First John 2:16, 17*

The Lord said, "If you do well, will not your countenance be lifted up? And if you do not do well, SIN is crouching at the door and its desire is for you; and you must master it." *Genesis 4:7*

Deception led me to base my life on the inaccurate belief of "Once Saved, Always Saved", OSAS. The Bible clearly teaches us this belief is inaccurate. I will be the first one to admit it is a catchy phrase! Satan has used it to deceive many people, me being one of them. When I believed OSAS applied to me, Satan deceived me and I lost sight of my own accountability and responsibility to live in obedience to God.

My false belief said, "Why worry about staying on the narrow path since nothing can keep you out of heaven now?" If OSAS is factual, then that gives each of us a license to live in sin, having no sin accounted to us. If OSAS is accurate, we would be free to participate in deeds of darkness doing whatever 'feels good' at the time, regardless of God's eternal rules. We could enter Heaven on a technicality, even if we chose to blaspheme and denounce the Lord later in life! OSAS is deceptive. My proof is the fact that I was truly saved in 1962 and truly saved in 1991 and I was truly lost somewhere in between.

The Bible confirms that we do have the right to hold onto or let go of, the perfect gift of Salvation. The following Scriptures are sound Biblical teachings on the matter.

> If we deliberately keep on sinning after we have received the knowledge of the truth, no sacrifice for sins is left, but only a fearful expectation of judgment and of raging fire that will consume the enemies of God. Anyone who rejected the Law of Moses died without mercy on the testimony of two or three witnesses. How much more severely do you think a man deserves to be punished who has trampled the Son of God under foot, who has

treated as an unholy thing the blood of the covenant that sanctified Him and who has insulted the Spirit of grace? For we know Him who said, "It is mine to avenge; I will repay," and again, "The Lord will judge his people. It is a dreadful thing to fall into the hands of the living God." *Hebrews 10:26-31*

"The Lord is with you when you are with Him. And if you seek Him, He will let you find Him, but if you forsake Him, He will forsake you." *Second Chronicles 15:2*

In my own unawareness, how often I remarked, "I may not be a very good Christian, but I am a Christian." The word, ignorance, comes to my mind when I think back to when I made that remark. I was deceived and I was lost. I wanted to live by my own rules, not God's rules, yet dare to think that I would go to Heaven when I died. Did I really think there was a safe middle ground between Heaven and hell? We cannot have it all here on earth and have it all there in Heaven. How foolish I was to think so immaturely and so inaccurately.

What I have said is truth but it is not a popular truth among many Christians. A vast number of people enjoy playing what I refer to as the GOD GAME. That game makes less sense than Russian Roulette. I will not get to Heaven by being a Christian On Sunday Only (COSO) who lives according to his own rules, especially the most comfortable and convenient ones the rest of the week.

A COSO is interested in acting like a Christian more than being a Christian. A genuine Christian strives and struggles to live by God's rules living every day, in every way, sold out to Jesus Christ. They are constantly concerned about how closely they are aligned with God's rules especially when no one else is looking. Complacency is deceptive and is devastating to the Christian lifestyle. Here is what the Scriptures teach us about falling away from God. Scripture does not lie for it is God's Word and it cannot lie.

> Enter by the narrow gate; for the gate is wide, and the way is broad that leads to destruction, and many are those who enter by it. For the gate is small and the way is narrow that leads to life, and few are those who find it. *Matthew 7: 13-14*

Therefore dear friends, since you already know this, be on your guard so that you may not be carried away by the error of lawless men and fall from your secure position, but grow in the grace and knowledge of our Lord and Savior, Jesus Christ. *2 Peter 3:17-18*

By this gospel, you are saved, if you hold firmly to the Word I preached to you. Otherwise, you have believed in vain. *I Corinthians 15:2*

So, if you think you are standing firm, be careful that you do not fall! *First Corinthians 10:12*

Once you were alienated from God and were enemies in your minds because of your evil behavior. Now He has reconciled you by Christ's physical body through death to present you holy in His sight, without blemish and free from accusation- if you continue in your faith, established and firm, not moved from the hope held out in the gospel. *Colossians 1:21*

> Therefore, my brothers, be all the more eager to make your calling and election sure. For if you do these things, you will never fall, and you will receive a rich welcome into the eternal kingdom of our Lord and Savior Jesus Christ. *Second Peter 1:10-11*

It appears that my realizing and admitting the state of my own sinful condition was the first step to receiving the spiritual cure that only Jesus could give me. Very soon after that realization came, God's hand moved in mysterious ways. He allowed me to fall by my own will, and then He lifted me up from my fallen position!

If you recognize yourself as having erroneously bought into either one or both of the common Christian mistaken beliefs: OSAS (Once Saved Always Saved) and COSO (Christian On Sunday Only), take heart! If you admit and repent of these sinful errors, help and healing will gradually overtake you and erase your errors!

8

There is no more confused message that you and I could give to a lost and dying world than to live in sin and at the same time to tell people about the transforming power of Jesus Christ. There is not a more confusing thing we can do to our kids, the generation behind us and to this world. God will not use a compromised life to reach a compromised world. God will use a life that is given over to Him, that is a demonstration of the message that through the power of Jesus Christ and His love, He can transform our lives and set us free. ~ Joe Focht*

*Joe Focht is Senior Paster of Calvary Chapel in Philadelphia, PA

When We Repent

A day in May of 1991 stands out vividly in my mind. It was the time of miraculous change in my spirit and in my life. It was when I surrendered, and Jesus saved me! I had ignored God and made Him second in my life for many years. I had actually fallen away from God, back sliding more and more as time progressed. I am very thankful that He did not give up on me. God had a plan for my life and a purpose for me.

God implemented His plan when He mercifully removed my ability to sleep for a period of several months. Sleep deprivation is a debilitating malady and it was a most effective tool for getting my attention. Even the most stubborn person and the most rebellious attitude can be broken when the gift of sleep vanishes for weeks and months on end. It was a silent and invisible torture. I am living proof of that!

I knew something was wrong one day when making a simple phone call became a complex task for me. I tried repeatedly to place a call while sitting at my desk and I dialed the number carefully but to no avail. A secretary walked into my office at that time and looked at me with a curious expression on her face. She kindly brought to my attention the fact that I was dialing the numbers on the calculator instead of my phone. I felt emotionally unstable and confused, wondering how I managed to drive to work in my sleep deprived state of mind.

I dreaded nighttime. I had never known such frustration! The inability to doze off and the lack of recuperative sleep affected me severely, placing me in a state of serious mental and physical decline. One evening, I climbed into bed on the wrong side because I did not remember which side of the bed I slept on. Familiar items sitting on the nightstand by the bed would have tipped off a rationally thinking person. I was oblivious to my surroundings. How I functioned in those days remains a mystery to me.

There came the day when I got lost on my way home from work. I felt as if I had ended up in some strange city on an unfamiliar road. I had no idea where I was. I saw nothing that looked vaguely familiar. I was no longer in control of my life or me. Ironically, I never was really in charge. I only thought I was in charge. The following verses illustrate the truth of Who really is in control of our lives.

THE HEALING BRUSH

My life was a canvas, unblemished, unstained; constant harmonious hues,

Until one day, I took the brush into my own hand and began to paint.

Immediately the colors smeared the canvas beyond recognition.

Once again, the canvas is a masterpiece because I finally placed

The brush of my life back in God's hand.

By Janet Rumpf [10]

Looking back, I clearly see God's orchestration of circumstances, His sense of patience and His demonstration of merciful love. His infinite wisdom and His ingenious plan was quite remarkable. Perhaps He shook His head slowly in bewilderment as He looked at me, while I drove that day. Perhaps I looked like a frightened goose in a hailstorm, not knowing which way to go. I believe it was the Holy Spirit that prompted me, for at that time I inquired aloud, "Lord, will You give me

10

a desire to return to You?"   (This little one line prayer was the signal to God that I was ready to wave the white flag of surrender and He responded mercifully!)

> For it is written, "As I live, says the Lord, every knee shall bow to Me, and every tongue shall give praise to God." *Romans 14:11*

How relieved I was to see a recognizable street sign as I slowly regained my senses. I could almost hear my Heavenly Father saying in His stern voice, "Pay attention Faye. You are in serious trouble. I will show you the way if you will listen to Me and do exactly what I tell you to do."

God never begs us to change. God does not force us to change. He does not order us to serve Him. His guiding hand was always reaching out to me, but I had to reach out to Him and place my trusting hand in His hand. I had to surrender my will, admitting and acknowledging that His way was the right way and my way was the wrong way. In the surrendering process, I believe that the sincere silent cry of the heart for God is as important as the verbal repentance from our lips.

We should endeavor to both feel and speak our sincere repentance and desire for our Creator's presence in our lives.

Only days after that episode, I willingly gave in. Suddenly, I found myself on my knees beside the bed alone with God. Unashamedly, weeping like a little girl, I cried out to the only Father I had ever known on earth, my Heavenly Father.

> I said, "Lord, please forgive me of my sins. I turn away from my rebellious life and give myself to You alone, Jesus. If You will come into my heart as Lord and Savior, I will serve You for the rest of my life. I will do whatever You tell me to do and I will go wherever You send me. From this moment on, I am Yours." Amen.

A wave of relief flowed through me like a cleansing flood washing away everything that had been inharmonious in my lifetime so far! I sensed God's presence; I felt a warm blanket of love, cascading over me, as if it was dropped from above. It covered all of me.

Minutes later, I stood up and walked down the hall past a mirror on the wall. I glanced at my reflection as I passed by the mirror. What I saw stopped me in my tracks. My eyes! I did not recognize the eyes looking back at me!

I stood very still and studied my own eyes. I saw love, kindness and compassion looking at me from somewhere within my new self and fresh sense of comprehension. Those eyes made me think of Jesus and I knew the Holy Spirit was on the inside of me! I had not seen those eyes in a long time! God supernaturally changed me in a matter of minutes!

> Jesus said, "The Son of Man did not come to be served, but to serve, and to give His life as a ransom for many."
> *Matthew 20:28*

My life was never the same after that day. Jesus saved me from sin and from hell. He changed me! By no means do I claim to be perfect, for I am not. I admit that sometimes I struggle and fail. Some days I feel myself fighting temptations and under pressure to do what I know is less than pleasing according to God's rules. However, I can honestly say that I strive to be what God wants me to be. When I fall short, I am quick to seek forgiveness. My life is now a life of humility, recognizing the fact that, God is everything and I am nothing in comparison. I understand that Jesus Christ by way of the cross is the only way to God the Father and to Heaven!

> Jesus said, "I am the way, the truth and the life. No one comes to the Father except through Me." *John 14:6*

9

Our natural inclination is to be so precise,
trying always to forecast accurately what will
happen next. As soon as we abandon ourselves
to God and do the task He has placed before
us, He begins to fill our lives with surprises.
The spiritual life is the life of a child. Leave
everything to Him and it will be gloriously
and graciously uncertain how He will come
in, but you can be certain that He will come.[11]
~ Oswald Chambers

11

Love Never Fails

The memorable summer in 1991 when I was born again was also the summer when I fell in love with Jesus. I had experienced falling in love with my husband but never with Jesus. Loving One I could not see with my eyes changed me. What I am saying will sound strange to you if you do not know Jesus as your Savior, if you have never fallen in love with Him in a spiritual sense. Words cannot describe what the experience is like. It is perfect love; it is an eternal love with One to whom we can entrust our secrets. For centuries, men and women have fallen in love with the Savior; it is a pure and unique love.

After I gave my heart to Jesus, I developed an insatiable appetite for the Word. (In 1970, I read the Word because I was compelled to read it. In 1991, I read the Word because I could not keep from reading it.) I fell in love with it, with the understanding that the Word is the mind of God.

For as long as I could remember, there had been a gnawing emptiness in my heart; I searched unsuccessfully for ways to fill the void. For the first time in my adult life, the emptiness vanished! Jesus and the Words in the Bible filled the void! When it happened, I could no longer recall what it was like not having Jesus in my heart. That thought was unthinkable.

Each line I read from the Bible was like soothing balm to my soul. No words can adequately describe the holy completion I experienced. The Words from the Bible seemed so familiar to me as if I knew them by heart, from another place and another time. Perhaps the words remained in my brain from the time I read them when I was seventeen. The emotion I felt surprised me in a good way.

Like lovely strands of pearls, the Holy Words poured into my hungry spirit, each word tumbling precisely into its own hewn crevice within my heart. For the first time, I understood that God's Words were alive!

I read the Bible every day that summer completing it in less than 90 days. I got up before sunrise each morning to pray and read the Word. When the Word saturated me, it affected me differently than it did when I read it in 1970. I realized God created a natural order to all things and firm rules, Heaven Rules, for us to live by and love by. The Word affected my comprehension in a deeper way than ever before and it filled me with love and the ability to love others.

> "And you shall love the Lord your God with all your heart, and with all your soul, and with your entire mind, and with all your strength: this is the first commandment. *Mark 12:30*

The second commandment is this:

> "Love your neighbor as yourself." *Mark 12:31*

I discovered when I gave Jesus first place in my life, my personal life improved. When I looked at family members and friends through the eyes of Jesus, I saw them differently. I no longer saw their imperfections first and their attributes last. What I saw as faults and imperfections before, no longer registered mentally as negative characteristics.

One of the first qualities that emerged in me after my conversion was unconditional love. My judgmental attitude, my desire for perfection, my critical spirit and my know-it-all mind-set, all crumbled in the presence of my new ability to love unconditionally. My capacity to love God more deeply and to love others unconditionally changed me and my expectations of others drastically.

Up until 1991, I thought in human terms with human priorities. Most of us are constantly seeking love and acceptance from other humans. I desired a relationship and marriage to reassure myself that I was loveable, valuable and acceptable. I needed to have my self-worth validated. The what if question stayed in the back of my mind before I was saved in such a powerful manner that I now refer to it as my **conversion**. What if my husband dies or what if he decides he does not want to be married to me? How will I cope if 'this or that' happens? When I gave my life to Jesus, He filled me with a 'simple knowing' that He would always make a way for me if I would only trust Him.

> A cord of three strands is not quickly torn apart. *Ecclesiastes 4:12*

All successful love affairs must include Jesus making the marriage a holy-trio. A marriage without Jesus is a duo and the duo will struggle pitifully. At best, the duo is as fickle as a beach ball on the edge of a cliff, a partnership built on breakable rules and temporary promises, influenced by unpredictable emotions.

> Therefore, everyone who hears these words of Mine and acts upon them may be compared to a wise man who built his house upon the rock. And the rain descended and the floods came and the winds blew and burst against that house and yet it did not fall, for it had been founded upon the rock, and everyone who hears these words of Mine, and does not act upon them, will be like a foolish man, who built his house upon the sand. And the rain descended and the floods came and the winds blew, and burst against that house, and it fell, and great was its fall.
> *Matthew 7: 24-27*

In reality, 100% of all marriages end in death or divorce. Joy and pain are associated with all human love. Still, we strive to obtain what we desire and it often leads to failure and broken hearts. I believe we are looking for love in all the wrong places. We need to gain the perspective on our lives that comes from realizing we are the spiritual offspring of the Heavenly Father. We are spirits, sent from Heaven to earth to have human experiences. With that in mind, we need to seriously consider and abide by our Father's Heaven Rules in order to be truly fulfilled, prosperous, and successful! Jesus Christ is the glue that holds life together, whether we are in a union or single.

I believe it is humanly impossible to give or receive true love the way God intended it until we belong to Jesus Christ, the Word has saturated us and we are new creatures in Christ. Humans do not have the ability to love perfectly without Divine help. This is probably the reason some people claim to be incapable of loving at all.

In my early days of conversion, I desired a personal relationship with Jesus and I attempted to make Him my priority in life. Our personal relationship came into existence when I learned a supernatural truth. Prayer is our way of talking to God. The Bible (the Word) is how God talks to us. Doing those two things placed me in the midst of a conversation with the Lord. That is how we came to know each other, resulting in my personal relationship with Jesus!

A personal relationship with Jesus Christ is the result of praying and reading the Bible every day. It is available to everyone, male and female, adult and child. We must make the effort and the commitment in order to experience a personal relationship with Jesus. A Jesus-first relationship is a relationship you and I can depend on.

- Jesus will never leave us by death or divorce.

- He cannot be swayed, seduced or convinced to leave us.

- He cannot be enticed away by another person, by lust, good looks, emotions, money, greed or position.

- The Jesus-first relationship is the only relationship on earth that comes with a guarantee that it will last forever!

I am not saying we should avoid human relationships and marriage. A marriage between a man and a woman is a gift from God. I was incredibly blessed to have a marriage for 35 years! I am saying human relationships should be secondary to the relationship with Jesus Christ. Secondary relationships have the ability to work because of the Jesus-first relationship!

When Jesus became first in my life, I came to a realization that everything else in my life was secondary. Everybody and everything became secondary. With that realization, came perfect peace. Fear of death lost its hold on me. I no longer felt like the death of a loved one would destroy me. I comprehended that life on earth is temporary.

Following my conversion experience, I never loved my husband and children less; I actually loved them more. Having God as my number one priority gave me the assurance that death is not the end. It is merely a transition from earth to Heaven for the Christian. That realization gave me comfort and certainty that if my loved ones walked with Jesus on earth we would see each other in Heaven after this life ended.

> I am the resurrection and the life, those who believe in Me, even though they die, will live, and everyone who lives and believes in Me will never die."
> *John 11:25, 26*

Making God first in our lives is actually the wisest decision we can ever make. I love Jesus more than I love anyone or anything and I know that Jesus loves me. When God is first, we can live each day unafraid. On our worst days, we can face the tragedies in life, even if we have lost everyone and everything, because we still have the most important One. God will provide all that we need, no matter what we lose or encounter in this lifetime. In Heaven, we will find restoration of all the loved ones in Christ who have died before us. A marvelous future awaits us! Jesus is the Rock on which we stand.

10

*Faith is not some weak and pitiful emotion,
but is strong and vigorous confidence built
on the fact that God is holy love. Even though
you cannot see Him right now and cannot
understand what He is doing, you know Him.
Disaster occurs in your life when you lack the
mental composure that comes from establishing
yourself on the eternal truth that God is holy
love. Faith is the supreme effort of your life,
throwing yourself with abandon and total
confidence upon God.[12] ~ Oswald Chambers*

12

Faith Defies Logic

As a new convert, more than twenty years ago, I found myself eagerly searching for all God's promises in the Bible. I felt like a child at Christmas time! The turning of each page led me to another promise, as good as having my name on it! In addition, your name as well! That first summer, I discovered Scriptures and Truths that had been right in front of me all the time! I was so happy to encounter a completely different and new world that began to unfold before my eyes and all around me.

> Without faith, it is impossible to please God. *Hebrews 11:6*

> Now faith is the assurance of things hoped for, the conviction of things not seen. For by it the men of old gained approval. By faith, we understand that the worlds were prepared by the Word of God so that what is seen was not made out of things which are visible. *Hebrews 11:1, 2, 3*

I set out to learn all I could about the power of faith, and how I could acquire faith. Even though I did not completely understand faith, I knew I wanted faith to become more than just a word. I wanted faith to become so real and active that I could touch it with my hand and see it with my eyes! My heart's desire was for faith to change my life and me.

> Faith comes by hearing and hearing by
> the Word of God. *Romans 10:17*

It was that simple. All I had to do was read the Word (the Bible) and believe it. When I read that Scripture, faith made sense to me! I grasped the concept that mentally transferring the supernatural Words from the Bible into my spirit would cause an energy exchange and an alteration of my circumstances! I soon comprehended that having strong faith was more desirable and beneficial than possessing all the money or power in the world. The more I read the Bible, the more I wanted to read it.

One day, I went to the grocery store and loaded my grocery cart to the top. I guided the cart toward the checkout lane and suddenly, a compulsion came over me, almost causing me to abandon my groceries! That compulsion astounded me and I strongly desired to run home to be with the Lord in a quiet place, pouring over His Word and soaking up His loving presence!

I compare the emotion I felt for the Lord that day with the feelings of crazy love one feels when falling in love. God's love was not physical; it was invisible and it was nearly intoxicating! I comprehended the experience was holy, pure and right in the sight of God! I understood God was calling me and drawing me nearer to the place I should have been all along. I learned to refer to those times of supernatural bonding as moments of grace and times of amazing love with my Heavenly Father.

In search of faith, I advanced aggressively in my Scriptural search. I had a radiant moment when I found the following Bible verse. I realized God really could provide anything I ever needed, spiritually and materially, *if I believed He could.*

> My God shall supply all your needs according to His riches in glory in Christ Jesus. *Philippians 4:19*

I made up my mind to believe the Bible literally. The only way I could believe one Scripture was to believe all of the Scriptures because they were God's Words. God spoke the Scriptures to the prophets by way of the Holy Spirit so the Word was sound and trustworthy enough to build my life upon for eternity. No matter if the Bible had been translated and reshaped at the hands of men, suffering omissions and additions all through the years. I surmised the Holy Spirit was powerful enough to translate the Bible when I read it, causing me to receive the Word precisely the way God sent it centuries ago.

Here is an example of how powerful the Holy Spirit is and why I believe the Holy Spirit can and will translate the Bible accurately for us. Remember, on the day of Pentecost, as told in the second chapter of Acts in the New Testament, we find that the Holy Spirit came down like a 'violent and rushing wind' and it filled the house where the apostles were sitting. There appeared to them 'tongues as of fire' distributing themselves and resting on each person. They all began speaking in other tongues, as the Holy Spirit gave them utterance. When this happened, the multitude came together and they were bewildered because each one was hearing them speak in his own language.

Now there were people there that day from many nations and the people spoke many different languages. Isn't it amazing how the Holy Spirit acted as a translator and an interpreter that day? The following Scripture assures us that the Holy Spirit is indeed capable of translating words for us so that we may understand the words that appear foreign to us.

> How is it that we each hear them in our own language to which we were born? We hear them in our own tongues speaking of the mighty deeds of God! *Acts 2:8, 11*
>
> We walk by faith, not by sight. *Second Corinthians 5:7*

I found faith to be an exhilarating experience, leading me into an exciting new supernatural world! Living by faith can be costly and comes with many trials, but not as costly as NOT living by faith. Once I embraced faith, God proceeded to teach me like a child in kindergarten. At first, He wooed me with His presence and answered every single prayer. Later on, as my education progressed and matured, He stepped back, to see if I would hold fast to Him, in spite of what I saw or did not see. Faith is not intellectual understanding; faith is a deliberate commitment to Jesus Christ, even when we cannot see the way we are going.

In the years that followed, my family and I endured many physical attacks against our bodies in the way of illnesses. We responded each time by faith, praying for healing and deliverance, believing it would come. I learned to find the corresponding Scriptures and promises that applied to a particular situation. I then decided to confess those Scriptures, speaking the Words aloud and keeping right on believing no matter what my eyes saw or my mind thought.

There were times when we received supernatural healing for our bodies and God demonstrated His power in incredible ways! We saw the results of faith with our own eyes! Both our children experienced supernatural healings; medical professionals verified those incidents. God evidenced Himself to me in dreams, visions and spoken words. I shared the details of many incidents in a previous book called,   A FAX FROM HEAVEN, condensed version.

My faith grew because of all the signs and wonders. My faith-building learning experience was a process and God taught me many things during those days of trials and answers. When it came time to go through heart breaking trials where God chose to answer my prayers in ways other than what I expected, He strengthened me so I could endure. Hope became a treasured asset to me. Hope was born out of need and out of my love for God and my faith in God.

> Consider it all joy, my brethren, when you encounter various trials, knowing that the testing of your faith produces endurance. And let endurance have its perfect result, that you may be made perfect and complete, lacking in nothing. *James 1:2, 3, 4*

I remember reading a wonderful description of faith that adequately conveys how faith really works in us. I read it in a devotional called "Streams in the Desert."[13]

"There are three levels of faith in the Christian experience. The first is being able to believe only when we see some sign or have some strong emotion. Like Gideon, we feel the fleece and are willing to trust God if it is wet. This may be genuine faith but it is imperfect. It is continually looking to feelings or some other sign

13

instead of the Word of God. We have taken a great step toward maturity when we trust God without relying on our feelings. It is more of a blessing when we believe without experiencing any emotion.

While the first level of faith believes when our emotions are favorable, the second level of faith believes when all feelings are absent. The third level of faith transcends the other two, for it is faith that believes God and His Word when circumstances, emotions, appearances, people, and human reason all seem to urge something to the contrary. May God grant us faith to completely trust His Word, even when every other sign points the other way."

I am content, having staked my earthly life and my life eternal on faith in the God of Abraham, Isaac and Jacob. He is the only living God and He sent His son, Jesus Christ to earth to die on the cross for your sins and my sins.

> And Jesus said to them, "…truly I say to you, if you have faith as a mustard seed, you shall say to this mountain, 'Move from here to there,' and it shall move; and nothing shall be impossible to you." *Matthew 17:20*

Can the same great miracles be done today that were done many years ago? "Where is the God of Elijah? He is waiting for today's Elijah to call on Him! The greatest Old or New Testament saints who ever lived were on a level that is quite within our reach. The same spiritual force that was available to them, and the energy that enabled them to become our spiritual heroes, are also available to us. If we exhibit the same faith, hope and love they exhibited, we will achieve miracles as great as theirs. A simple prayer from our mouths will be powerful enough to call down from Heaven God's gracious dew or the melting fire of His spirit, just as the words from Elijah's mouth called down literal rain and fire. All that is required is to speak the words with the same complete assurance of faith with which he spoke."[14]

14

11

Hope is the thing with feathers—

That perches in the soul—

And sings the tune without the words—

And never stops—at all.

~ Emily Dickinson

We Have Hope

It was two in the morning and I still could not sleep. Christmas of 2011 was two weeks away and there was so much to do. It has never been easy for me to turn off my brain at night. That night in particular, many faces loomed in the forefront of my mind. As long as I can remember, I have had the desire to help others in some way and praying is one of the best ways. A prayer offered on behalf of any person is serious business. Each face was associated with a person's particular problem or painful situation. Each person I prayed for had specific needs yet each one had something in common. Every person was in need of the gift of hope!

I categorized the needs based on priorities, and spiritual needs were at the top of the list. Cures for diseases, healing for broken hearts, broken homes and fractured families fell second on the list. Prayers for those who were ill, lonely, grieving, misdirected, unemployed and in financial trouble followed. There seemed to be no stopping place.

God had answered numerous prayers all through the years, for which I was thankful. Too many prayers, however, had remained unanswered for a long time, years in some instances. I did not see why that was the case. Nothing is too difficult for the Lord. Although many of the needs were complex, I knew God could right every wrong. He could fix every tiny detail in each situation.

I sat in my kitchen in those early hours of the morning and I became very emotional about God's seemingly slow response and my lack of patience.

After what seemed like a very long time, I returned to bed. I did not know of any circumstantial changes at that moment but I had a strong assurance that in each case, there was still hope! With God, all things are possible and hope paved the way for amazing solutions and answers to materialize at any moment!

Hope is an amazing force! I still had God's promises on each matter and I had a holy expectation cemented by faith! I decided to keep on believing and standing firm, filled with anticipation! I had somehow allowed the miraculous reality of HOPE to diminish beneath the stack of prayer requests for which some answers and solutions seemed virtually impossible. I was praying for hope for others yet I allowed my sight to get in the way of my faith. I realized I too was in need of the gift of hope.

It had long been my belief that if we stop hoping, soon, we begin dying. I was in need of spiritual refreshment in the hope department! That is the case in the lives of so many people in this world. Satan unleashes his deluge of doubt, despair and discouragement on a regular basis. He slings it like a dripping wet paintbrush lifted from a can of paint, splattering the content on unsuspecting bystanders. The devil's attacks are known as SPIRITUAL WARFARE. Resistance is required to defeat the persistent enemy who longs to erase our hope or to cover it with a layer of hopelessness! Our weapons are spiritual weapons!

- Finally, be strong in the Lord and in the strength of His might. Put on the full armor of God, that you may be able to stand firm against the schemes of the devil.

- For our struggle is not against flesh and blood, but against the rulers, against the powers, against the world forces of this darkness, against the spiritual forces of wickedness in the heavenly places.

- Therefore, take up the full armor of God that you may be able to resist in the evil day and having done everything to stand firm. Stand firm therefore, having girded your loins with truth and having put on the breastplate of righteousness, and having shod your feet with the preparation of the gospel of peace.

- In addition to all, taking up the shield of faith with which you will be able to extinguish all the flaming missiles of the evil one, and take the helmet of Salvation and the sword of the Spirit which is the Word of God.

- With all prayer and petition pray at all times in the Spirit, and with this in view, be on the alert with all perseverance and petition for all the saints. (Ephesians 6:10-18)

We should stay in the habit of looking at the silver lining of storm clouds and not the storm. When God is involved, we should always expect Him to answer our requests in certainty. When we allow ourselves to get discouraged, suddenly, we become helpless souls. We lose our ability to pray for others and ourselves. When discouragement and despair come calling, instructing us to give up, lie down and die, that is the very time we have to stand up and stand firm! If we are children of God, we are not without hope! God has limitless resources! God has no limits and my lack of faith and hope are the only forces by which He is limited.

I reinvigorate my supply of hope by reading about God doing the impossible! It reminds me that God has all the power and because of His power, I will always have hope. When I pray and believe God will perform miracles in response to impossible situations and circumstances, He will do the impossible. Here are some of the times God did the impossible and He is the same today as He was then.

> When Elisha needed protection from the Aramean's plot to capture him, God sent horses and chariots of fire that filled the mountains around Elisha. They were from the spirit world and no one saw them except Elisha and his servant. God struck Elisha's adversaries with blindness to assure his safety.
> *Second Kings, Chapter 6*
>
> God's power remained strong in His servant Elisha, so that power remained in him after he died. Later, as a man was

being buried, his body touched Elisha's bones and the dead man revived and stood up on his feet. *Second Kings, Chapter 13*

In the books of Matthew and Acts, Scripture tells us how Jesus raised the dead, healed the sick and restored sight to the blind. A woman was healed when she only touched the hem of His garment! God performed extraordinary miracles by the hands of Paul! Handkerchiefs or aprons that Paul touched were carried to the sick. When touched by the cloth, they were healed and evil spirits came out of them.

Sometimes we forget about God's power that can accomplish anything, absolutely anything! We should never underestimate God's power! Reading a couple of reminders always helps me regroup and regain my courage, my faith and my hope!

The well-known writer, L. B. Cowman told an amazing story that I love to recall! One day in autumn, she was out on the open prairie and she saw an eagle that had been mortally wounded by a rifle shot. His eyes were still gleaming like small circles of light and he slowly turned his head, giving one last searching and longing look toward the sky. He had often swept those starry spaces with his wonderful wings. The beautiful sky was the home of his heart. It was his domain. In those lofty heights, he had raced the wind and played with lightening a thousand times. Suddenly, death was upon him because just once, he forgot, and flew too low. My soul is that eagle. This is not my home. It must never lose its skyward look. I must keep my faith and I must keep my hope. I must keep my courage and I must keep Christ! It would be better to crawl from the battlefield than to not be brave. There is no time for my soul to retreat.[15]

I must never take my eyes off the sky, the high places and the powerful source of my blessed hope!

15

For I know the plans that I have for you declares the Lord, plans for welfare and not for calamity to give you a future and a hope. *Jeremiah 29:11*

12

For glory befits God because of His majesty,

while lowliness befits man because

it unites us with God. ~ St. Diadochos

Blue Sky

My simple childhood life, in Holmes County, Mississippi was free from the complexities of excessive belongings. I climbed trees, roamed the woods in bare feet, picked berries and fished with a cane pole. I had an abundance of curiosity causing me to question what was beyond the horizon, where the sun went at night and how far away Heaven was. I needed to know how many stars were in the sky. I believed I could soar in the sky like a bird if I could run fast enough with outstretched arms. I never once got airborne but that never stopped me from trying!

My very first significant memory in life happened when I was only three years old. One cool, crisp autumn day, I awoke from an afternoon nap and found myself lying on the ground between two rows of cotton stalks. My head rested on a small partially filled sack of cotton. In every direction, all I saw was cotton stalks. I could not see over them or through them. I was frightened at first by the aloneness and silence except for the cawing of a crow.

Suddenly, the cotton stalks grew strangely dim and I looked up into a canopy of the most beautiful blue sky that one could ever imagine! As soon as I looked up, I felt an awesome presence descending on me. The blue sky came alive to me!

I did not see a face or eyes looking back at me but I knew without a doubt that something or someone was up there looking back at me. Whatever it was, it made me feel happy, safe and loved. I stood still for a few moments before calling out to Mama. She answered me from a distance. I ran through the cotton field, following the sound of Mama's voice, smiling broadly and glancing upward towards Heaven as I ran!

Many years passed before I understood what actually happened that day. That special day was the very first time God revealed Himself to me and demonstrated His love for me.

> Oh Lord, Thou dost know when I sit down and when I rise up.
>
> Thou dost understand my thought from afar. Thou dost scrutinize my path and my lying down, and art intimately acquainted with all my ways. Even

before there is a word on my tongue,
behold, oh Lord, Thou dost know it all.

If I take the wings of the dawn, if I dwell
in the remotest part of the sea, even
there, Thy hand will lead me. *Psalms
139: 1-12, 24*

More than fifty years later, I came to an intense
awareness that GOD manifested Himself to me as a
three year old by a powerful means. He allowed me
to see Him as Blue Sky! From that understanding,
I also comprehended that God was everywhere.
There is nowhere we can go to escape His presence.
The realization caused me to sit still, pondering the
significance of the profound awareness. The knowledge
had always been there; I had never accessed, processed
or comprehended it before.

I thought back to the time I was three, the day the
blue sky came down to me in that Mississippi cotton
field. Blue sky seemed very much alive and it fell on me
like a gentle breeze; only the breeze flowed vertically
instead of horizontally.

I was taken aback when I understood that God is
in every single molecule in the universe! God has the

ability to be in one place in one form. At the same time, He can be everywhere in the universe, like scattered molecules of the gases of the atmosphere!

God seems to manifest Himself in different ways to different people according to their particular needs at the time. He can reveal specific attributes of Himself to us such as Light, Love, and Peace, for example. I had heard from numerous people who stated they saw tiny sparkling particles of light surrounding them in times of crisis in their lifetimes. God was there! I recalled my own personal experience, when I was a child in an automobile accident.

As the car rolled repeatedly, I distinctly remember seeing small sparkling particles of light. They were everywhere, as plentiful as feathers from a pillow, surrounding us in the form of a protective barrier, like molecules of the gases of the atmosphere. God was in that car with us that day! God is Light.

> "Am I a God who is near," declares the Lord, "And not a God far off? Can a man hide himself in hiding places, so I do not see him? Do I not fill the heavens and the earth?" declares the Lord. *Jeremiah 23:23, 24*

My thoughts raced back to conversations I had with two people from different parts of the country. I had interviewed a man from Colorado and a woman from Tennessee before including their stories in my first book. The woman, Jacque, told of a near-death-experience after being electrocuted. The man, Bart, told of a near-death-experience after a closed head injury. They talked about blue mist and blue sky. What they described was like blue molecules in the atmosphere. The man spoke of breathing in the blue mist, breathing in love. God is love!

> Jacque said, "I cannot describe the peace I felt. All fear left me; I had no regrets or anxious thoughts. There was only peace. I looked up into that lovely blue sky and I saw one billowy, cumulous-looking cloud. The distance between the cloud and me was closing in. I could not tell if the cloud was descending toward me or if I was ascending toward the cloud!" God is peace!

The cloud was three-dimensional. The part of the cloud that extended closest to me was the purest white I had ever seen. Shades of dark blue, unlike the blue-sky background, rimmed the cloud and resembled a transparent blue mist. Knowledge was imparted to me, allowing me to comprehend that Jesus was in the cloud coming for me. I was dying and Jesus gave me the intellectual capacity to know that. I was not afraid." [16]

> Bart said, "It's like trying to describe a roller coaster ride. As you describe it, you can feel it. I have said many times, I do not have the words in my vocabulary to describe the awesomeness of what happened to me. I do not know those words. It is beyond my vocabulary to speak of it. All I can do is make analogies. I could feel, I could taste, and I could hear, I could smell; I was using all my senses and I could feel the love.

The love was alive. It was a light blue mist. There was love all around me. It was just there. I do not know

16

where it came from or where it went. It was just there; and it was overwhelming. I was experiencing love through all my senses, and I was actually breathing in love."[17]

> The one who does not love does not know God, for God is love. *I John 4:8*

When I was three years of age, I called God Blue Sky and perhaps that is how I will always see Him. Each time I lift my eyes to the Heavens I see His vastness, His grandeur, His splendor. At the same time, I see His personal touch and His thoughtfulness to tiny details. I will never forget the attention He showed me as a small waking child. That day God was Blue Sky!

> Such knowledge is too wonderful for me. It is too high; I cannot attain to it. *Psalms 139:6*

> For My thoughts are not your thoughts, neither are your ways My ways, declares the Lord. For as the heavens are higher than the earth, so are My ways higher

17

than your ways and My thoughts than your thoughts. *Isaiah 55:8-9*

One day, I sat in the reception area in the office of a dentist, patiently awaiting my turn in the chair. I watched a tiny gold fish swimming in the peaceful water within the confines of the aquarium. I smiled to myself thinking, "I am the goldfish and God is the water".

In Him we live, move, and have our being. *Acts 17:28*

All that I do, think or say, He knows. All that I am, He is aware of it. There is no way I can separate myself from Him, nor do I wish to.

For I am convinced that neither death nor life, nor angels nor principalities, nor things present, nor things to come, nor powers, nor height, nor depth, nor any other created thing shall be able to separate us from the love of God, which is in Christ Jesus our Lord. *Romans 8:38-39*

God is everywhere for He is Omnipresent. The world and universe is His Church for God cannot be contained in a building with walls. He fills every square inch of His vast creation so I can be sure that He knows when I am behaving in or out of harmony with His Heaven Rules. God hears my laughter, sees my tears, recalls, and records every word I have ever thought or said. He is there with you now and He is here with me now. God is Omnipresent, Omnipotent and Omniscient!

> "But will God indeed dwell on the earth? Behold heaven and the highest heaven cannot contain Thee, how much less this house which I have built!" *First Kings 8:27*

God implemented surveillance of humankind long before humankind implemented surveillance of humankind. God has on hand a video of your life and my life from conception until death. I have forgotten many things I have done and said. God has not forgotten even one thing. The very thought of that should be enough to inspire us to change our behavior into conformity with that of the Saints.

13

I have come home at last! This is my real country! I belong here. This is the land I have been looking for all my life, though I never knew it till now...Come further up, come further in!"

~ C.S. Lewis

Heaven

Everything I have written in this book thus far was written intentionally, in an attempt to guide others and myself in the right direction. My strong desire is to encourage all of us to become sturdy spiritual beings that will one day live with Jesus in Heaven eternally. Whatever we do, say and think shapes our minds and our souls. The spiritual forces we invite into our lives and gravitate towards will build us up or tear us down and ultimately usher us into eternity. Heaven is a real place!

My sister lived near Mobile, Alabama and had for many, many years. In 1977, she was in a very serious car collision a short distance from her home and she died, briefly, because of the accident. When her spirit left her body, she entered a tunnel and she knew she was not alone in the tunnel. She did not see who it was that accompanied her as they began the incredibly fast ascent through the tunnel flying toward a source of brilliant white light! She found comfort in the fact that she was not alone. Barbara suddenly started breathing again very shortly after she died and she lived to describe what she saw in those brief moments in the Heavenly realm when her spirit left her body.

Barbara said while she was in the tunnel, she had absolutely no pain, but an extraordinary sense of amazing well being! She felt peace! She arrived at the end of the tunnel and she was convinced she was home in Heaven! Barbara sounded sad when she told how in an instant, she was back in her body in excruciating pain from a severe head injury, a broken neck and fractured collarbone. Once again, she found herself in a hospital bed in a small room in Singing River Hospital in Pascagoula, Mississippi.

The Bible and those who have been to Heaven via 'near-death' experiences describe Heaven as a marvelous place! Those 'time-travelers' who lived to tell what they saw said Heaven was pleasing to the soul, the eyes and ears and all the senses. Those who have been there did not want to leave because it was more spectacular than anything they ever imagined before or since.

Most of us let our minds dwell on Heaven more than hell because heavenly thoughts are typically beautiful and pleasing. Hell thoughts are predictably ugly and unpleasant. A close review of the Bible makes it clear that Heaven is an extraordinary place and hell is an unbearable place. I firmly believe we should contemplate the reality of Heaven and hell daily. We should live our lives as if we could be in one of those two places in the twinkling of an eye!

Here is what the Bible has to say about Heaven. The Apostle John was on the Island of Patmos when the Lord appeared to him in a vision. The following Scripture is part of John's marvelous vision that was recorded in the book of Revelation.

> "And I saw a new Heaven and a new earth; for the first Heaven and the first earth passed away, and there is no longer any sea...Behold, the tabernacle of God is among men, and He shall dwell among them, and they shall be His people, and God Himself shall be among them. He shall wipe away every tear from their eyes, and there shall no longer be any death, there shall no longer be any mourning, or crying, or pain; the first things have passed away. He who overcomes shall inherit these things and I will be his God and he will be My son."
> *Revelation 21:1, 3, 4*

The foundation stones of the city wall were adorned with every kind of precious stone. The first foundation stone was jasper, the second, sapphire; the third, chalcedony; the fourth, emerald...and the twelve gates were twelve pearls, each one of the gates was a single pearl... the street of the city was pure gold, like transparent glass. ... The city had no need of the sun or of the moon to shine upon it, for the glory of God has illumined it, its lamp is the Lamb..., and nothing unclean and no one who practices abomination and lying shall ever come into it, but only those whose names are written in the Lamb's book of life.
Revelation 21:19, 20, 23, 27

NINETY MINUTES IN HEAVEN is a book written by Don Piper, a Baptist minister. It is a true story about a car accident that took his life. Don went to Heaven for an hour and a half before his spirit re-entered his body and he came back to earth. Don came back to earth but not because he wanted to. He preferred to remain in Heaven but God had other plans.

Don remarked that on earth, age expressed time passing; but in Heaven, there was no such thing as time. He recognized many of the people he encountered in heaven. Strangely, they were the same age they had been the last time he saw them. What Don encountered in that celestial paradise, amazed him. He noted that all the reminders of the aging process and the ravages of living on planet earth were erased from the faces of those people who had died and gone to heaven. Even though some of their features were not considered attractive on earth, in Heaven, those same features were lovely, perfect, beautiful and wonderful to look at.

Don said, "When I first stood in Heaven, they (the people I knew on earth) were in front of me and came rushing toward me. They embraced me and no matter which direction I looked I saw someone I had loved and who had loved me…I know what the Bible meant by perfect love. It emanated from every person who surrounded me…I felt as if I absorbed their love for me."

"Everything I saw glowed with intense brightness. A holy awe came over me as I stepped forward. I had no idea what lay ahead but I sensed that with each step I took it would grow more wondrous. Then I heard the music…Myriads of sounds filled my mind and heart and it is difficult to explain them. The most amazing one was the angel wings…a beautiful holy melody with a cadence that seemed never to stop. The swishing resounded as if it was a form of never-ending praise. The praise was unending but the most remarkable thing to me was that hundreds of songs were being sung at the same time, all of them worshiping God."[18]

I can only imagine how awesome it will be to enter that place! My gratitude will be immense, knowing that Jesus Christ died on a cross to deliver me from my sins. Jesus paid all the costs associated with my trip to Heaven and my living expenses for eternity! That special day when I enter Heaven is drawing nearer each minute and for all I know, it could come before I go to sleep this very night. That is why I try to walk in an upright manner before God each day. Who knows when He will call out, saying, "Come up now!" Be ready to depart at any given moment!

> When the son of Man (Jesus) comes in
> His glory and all the angels with Him,
> then He will sit on His glorious throne.
> All the nations will be gathered before
> Him and He will separate them from

18

one another, as the shepherd separates the sheep from the goats and He will put the sheep on His right and the goats on His left. Then the King will say to those on His right, "Come, you who are blessed of My Father, inherit the kingdom prepared for you from the foundation of the world". Then He will say to those on His left, "Depart from Me, accursed ones, into the eternal fire which has been prepared for the devil and his angels. And these will go away into eternal punishment, but the righteous into eternal life."
Matthew 25:31-34, 41, 46

14

The buck stops here. ~ Harry Truman

Hell

Since I started writing books about near-death experiences, after-death appearances and miraculous occurrences, I have been able to engage in conversations with many people who claim they have firsthand knowledge of Heaven following a near-death experience. I find it captivating to listen to actual accounts from those who have died, been resuscitated and lived. I find it worthy of note that we hear far more about positive Heavenly experiences than we do about negative hell experiences from those time-travelers who have been to the other side and back.

We as human beings find it difficult to admit to failure, therefore, near-death experiences that generate hellish encounters are likely to remain hidden away in the recesses of the mind, never to be mentioned by the one who survived the near-death experience. I am grateful that a few survivors have bravely told about the hell they encountered when they died, before they received resuscitation.

I have written the previous chapter and this chapter to draw attention to the fact that both Heaven and hell exist, no matter what we read in the newspapers or hear on television to the contrary. Based on Biblical teachings and firsthand accounts provided by those who have lived to tell their to hell and back stories, hell is wretched and miserable. Hell cannot be ignored and the subject should not be avoided, dismissed or considered inappropriate.

As for hell and the person who sees no wrong in sin and rebellion toward God, here is what the Bible tells us.

> "But for the cowardly and unbelieving and abominable and murderers and immoral persons and sorcerers and idolaters and all liars, their part will be in the lake that burns with fire and brimstone, which is the second death."
> *Revelation 21:7, 8*

Dr. Charles Garfield, a respected researcher of near-death experiences and author of BETWEEN LIFE AND DEATH, noted, "Not everyone dies a blissful, accepting death...Almost as many of the dying patients interviewed reported negative visions (demons and so forth), as reported blissful experiences, while some reported both."[19]

In 1948, for example, George Godkin of Alberta, Canada related a despairing near-death affair in the midst of a prolonged illness:

"I was guided to the place in the spirit world called hell. This is a place of punishment for all those who reject Jesus Christ. I not only saw hell, but also felt the torments that all who go there will experience.

The darkness of hell is so intense that it seems to have a pressure per square inch. It is an extremely black, dismal, desolate, heavy, pressurized type of darkness. It gives the individual a crushing, despondent feeling of loneliness.

The heat is a dry, dehydrating type. Your eyeballs are so dry they feel like red-hot coals in the sockets. Your tongue and lips are parched and cracked with the intense heat. The breath from your nostrils as well as the air you breathe feels like a blast from a furnace. The exterior of your body feels as though it were encased within a white-hot stove. The interior of your body has a sensation of scorching hot air being forced through it. The agony and loneliness of hell cannot be expressed

19

clearly enough for proper understanding to the human soul; it has to be experienced."[20]

The description above is horrific but it pales in comparison to the reality and true horrors of hell that are unbearable and unthinkable! The fact that the misery never ends, the separation from God is permanent, the depression and despair from which hell dwellers can never escape forces me to look closely at the matter.

God does not want us to go to hell but He in His infinite wisdom offers us free will and individual choices. Why would He want us to be in Heaven if we do not want to be there? If the saved and the lost all go to Heaven, as many naïve people have convinced themselves, surely chaos would ensue there. Heaven would resemble our present day circumstances where streets are not safe to walk in many places. Our earthly moral decay has led us to a present day society of participants caught up in undeniable battles of good versus evil; consequentially we have overflowing jails and prisons and increasing hopelessness.

> In Second Peter 3:9, we read, "The Lord is not slow about His promises, as some

20

count slowness, but is patient toward you, not wishing for any to perish but for all to come to repentance."

One of the most fascinating near-death experiences I have ever heard of happened in the summer of 1848. Perhaps I was intrigued by this account because of the purity of the story. The woman who experienced the vision of Heaven and hell lived in another place and time. She had no outside influences such as television, movies, books or talk shows to color and shape the holy vision she saw. I believe her story is the most accurate humanly spoken description I have ever encountered that describes what really exists beyond our world.

Marietta was born in 1823 in Berlin, New York. She became very ill when she was only 25 years of age and she entered a comatose state. She did not respond to the attempts made by her family or her physician who all tried to rouse her. After being in an unconscious state for nine days, Marietta regained consciousness and began relaying details of where she had been and what she saw during the nine-day period. I believe her assessment of hell was more accurate than I ever could have imagined!

Here are some of Marietta's statements about her hell experience that affected my perception of hell permanently. Marietta spoke, saying:[21]

- My mind was flooded with horror and despair. I was horror-struck.

- If only I could have one hour back on earth to make myself fit for Heaven.

- Not one of my secrets was hidden. They were all there.

- I reeled in turmoil, longing to escape.

- I fell rapidly and the surrounding darkness opened to receive me.

- Crowds of spirits gathered beneath the foliage and sparkling vegetation. The whole scene seemed to be artificial, gaudy, tinselly playacting.

- The phosphorescent glare burned my eyes. The fruit scorched my hand and seared my lips as I tried to eat.

- The air was laden with disappointment and misery.

21

- The spray from the fountain was like drops of molten lead.

- I heard voices, bursts of laughter, shouts of revelry, witty ridicule. There were obscenities, horrible curses, degrading propositions, backbiting, polished sarcasm, hollow compliments, and pretended congratulations.

- The trees blossoms were the sparkle of relentless flames. Each object caused me agony as I approached it.

- One spirit said, "Delicious fruit, I can never taste. Refreshing air, I can never feel and peaceful sleep I can never enjoy. My desires are so unnatural that the very things I crave I detest and the things I delight in torture me."

- Another said, "Here you find lust and pride, hatred, greed, strife, love of self, blasphemies all fanned into a raging fire. The total effect is the combination of every evil. Now we have fallen into this fearful place. We have caused our own sorrow. God is just. He is good. We know this state we are in is not the result of a vindictive law of God. This misery came about by our own breaking the moral law."[22]

22

God does not want anyone to be lost. You and I will choose our own destinations. God does not want us to go into eternal punishment. In spite of His great love for us, however; He is not going to force us to serve Him.

Marietta concluded her impression of Hell by saying she had learned much. She discovered that deceit is the foundation of darkness and the source of much trouble. It is a camouflage to hide the consequences of lying and evil. In addition to this, she clearly saw that no deception, no matter how cleverly fabricated, could conceal truth on the final day when everything is tested.[23]

> Realize this, that in the last days difficult times will come. For men will be lovers of self, lovers of money, boastful, arrogant, revilers, disobedient to parents, ungrateful, unholy, unloving, irreconcilable, malicious gossips, without self-control, brutal, haters of good, treacherous, reckless, conceited, lovers of pleasure rather than lovers of God, holding to a form of godliness, although they have denied its power;

23

and avoid such men as these. *Second Timothy 3:1-5*

Consider what Dr. Maurice Rawlings wrote in his book, 'TO HELL AND BACK'. "If there is a hell, if the Bible is true...then we must each decide for ourselves, is it safe to die? Intriguing the mind and baffling the soul, it is perhaps one of life's most important questions. The answer lies no more than a few heartbeats away.[24]

> Do not be conformed to this world, but be transformed by the renewing of your mind, that you may prove what the will of God is, that which is good and acceptable and perfect." Romans 12:2 "According to His (Jesus) promise we are looking for new heavens and a new earth, in which righteousness dwells. Therefore, beloved, since you look for these things, be diligent to be found by Him in peace, spotless and blameless. *Second Peter 3:14-15*

24

15

The important thing is not to stop questioning. Curiosity has its own reason for existing. Never lose a holy curiosity. ~ Albert Einstein

Discernment

Very simply stated, discernment is the ability to decide between truth and error, between right and wrong. Discernment is the process clarifying our thinking about Biblical truth. When I think with discernment, I am subjecting my thoughts and actions to the scrutiny of the Word of God.

> Examine everything carefully, hold fast to that which is good; abstain from every form of evil. *First Thessalonians 5:21-22*

The believer is required to exhibit discretion in every area of life. God's Word provides us with the needed discernment to make wise personal choices and decisions in school, college, at home and in the work place.

How necessary discernment is to every move, choice and decision we make, especially in places   where we tend to think we need no discernment, where we are inclined to let our guard down. Discernment is essential when considering where we should worship and which preacher we should believe. I write the following paragraphs for the benefit of the new converts.

Many wonderful churches and clergy are in the world today. Countless leaders are devoted and actively promoting the Word of truth according to an enlightened understanding of the Bible. Genuine churches play a positive role in the lives of Christians.

Sadly, however, charlatans create some churches; they are just buildings open for business. The word church is not synonymous with God. False preachers are standing in many pulpits pretending to be the real deal and they open church doors to unsuspecting churchgoers. They shape gullible parishioners into a misguided flock by teaching their own distorted opinions instead of Biblical truth. The conclusion is, not all churches are good. Good and evil exists in every sector of life. There is unprecedented instability within the pastoral community. Churches are only as holy as the humans who occupy the buildings.

A recent survey showed alarming statistics. We should consider these statistics and assume responsibility for our own walk with Christ. Pastors are only human and we cannot blame pastors for our spiritual inadequacies. 18 years of researching pastoral trends throughout the United States, showed preaching was the most stressful and frustrating working profession, even more than doctors, lawyers and politicians. 89% of pastors surveyed considered leaving ministry. 57% said they would leave if they had a better place to go-including secular work. 77% felt they were unqualified to lead. 72% of pastors surveyed said they ONLY studied the Bible when preparing sermons. Only 23% felt happy and content with who they are in Christ.[25]

It is interesting that in the world today, we find numerous religions, denominations, doctrines and various teachers in leadership roles. In the absence of discretion and discernment, we could easily end up in a church that ironically leads people away from God. Some preach watered down Truth because many do not want to lose their church's tax-exempt status or their church members if the members are offended.

There are idol worshipers, atheists and agnostics poised to lead others astray. Some denominations condone same sex marriages and homosexuality in their

25

leadership and congregations, contradicting Biblical teachings. A recent trend combines Christianity with Islam, which is a strange and false religion. It is called "Chrislam" and it is an abomination. Those of the Islam faith do not worship the living God of Abraham, Isaac and Jacob as Christians do nor do they believe Jesus Christ is the Savior who died on the cross and bore our sins.

Some religions are devoted to Satan, witches and warlocks. These are just a few of the religious absurdities awaiting unsuspecting God seekers. It is safe to say that every religious action, statement and belief should be proven or disproven by the Holy Bible, the infallible Word of God, by discernment.

Bear in mind, there are those church leaders who have discovered it is easier to accept and condone sin than it is to reject and condemn sin. There are churchgoers who will only listen to preachers who "tickle their ears" and tell them what they want to hear. Hearing the truth may incite the anger of churchgoers who do not wish to hear the truth. Some churchgoers seek inconsistent pastors who are willing to be manipulated.

The Apostle Paul writes in Second Timothy 4:2, 3, 4. Preach the word; be ready in season and out of season, reprove, rebuke, exhort, with great patience and instruction. For the time will come when they will not endure sound doctrine, but wanting to have their ears tickled, they will accumulate for themselves teachers in accordance to their own desires, and will turn away their ears from the truth, and will turn aside to myths.

I believe that we who are living in the year of our Lord 2012 are sadly in that time. I emphasize the need for discernment in churches because in times of spiritual crisis, such as we as a nation are in today, many people seek God in churches, wrongly assuming all churches and all church leaders are a holy extension of God. Those assumptions could not be farther from the truth.

Each passing day reminds me that I need a personal relationship with Jesus Christ. A personal relationship with Jesus Christ comes as a result of accepting Jesus as Savior, then seeking God daily by prayer and meditating in His Holy Word. The Bible is God's way of talking to me, prayer is my way of talking to God, and the relationship comes as a result of spending that time with the Lord each day.

No one on this earth can accomplish this for me. By discernment, I know this is my own responsibility for which I will receive the consequences. In addition, the same applies to you. When my body grows hungry and weak, I must put food in my mouth and chew it then swallow it. No one can do this for me. When my spirit grows weak and ineffective, I must read the Bible and pray from my heart. No one can do this for me either. This falls under the heading of PERSONAL RESPONSIBILITY.

A woeful lack of personal responsibility and discernment can gravely pave the way for a whole nation to be terribly misaligned with God's compass. For example, in 1962, at the insistence of one woman, and then as a ruling by the Supreme Court of America, prayer and Bible reading was eliminated from our public schools. Since 1973, another ruling by the Supreme Court of America has allowed more than fifty-six million unborn babies to be murdered by abortion.[26] As of the present date, one abortion/murder happens every twenty seconds![27] Yes, "murder" is the correct word.

26
27

We also need to take personal responsibility, according to the Holy Spirit, in order to carefully discern the truth or error of the huge influence of the TV, Internet, and media in our lives. For example, are we really aware that society frequently uses vocabulary in order to control the minds of the masses?

It insidiously finds a positive name for something that is evil in order to get the masses to gradually adapt to and accept abominations. It calls murder "choice." It calls homosexuality "gay," hopeless drinking parties "happy hours," garbage humor "adult humor," and pornography, "adult entertainment." Society habitually turns its back on the wisdom from this clearly stated Holy Scripture:

> Woe unto them that call evil good and good evil; that put darkness for light, and light for darkness; that put bitter for sweet, and sweet for bitter! *Isaiah 5:20*

"Are we vigilantly watching the gradual erosion of Truth in our nation and willing to listen to the Holy Spirit individually on how to take action to remedy the huge problem? It is a fact that God's rules of Eternal Truth, "The Ten Commandments" have gradually been removed from the walls of our cities and institutions of learning. Our rights to pray in public and in some cases to even speak the words, "God Bless you" have been extinguished. These are all consequences, for WE as a nation have shamefully turned our backs on God and His laws. Even the Highest Court in the land has followed suit. We have denied His name. Do we dare to wonder why we are in very deep trouble now as a nation?

Our nation can be compared to the ship, "The Titanic." We as individuals, with few exceptions, are partying on the boat, totally unaware of the potential danger, destruction, and calamity that we are slowly but surely moving toward. Several strong, loud cries of "warning" are being sounded by the modern day prophets of our nation, even as you read this. You who have ears to hear please listen and respond. The fate of this "Titanic" ship and its passengers rest in your hands."[28]   At this very moment you, personally, are being called upon to quickly respond according to our Maker's Heaven Rules!

28

As stated previously, it is not by accident or chance that you are reading these very words at this moment in time and space. I believe that Jesus, the Son of the Living God, is personally knocking on the door of your individual heart. The King of Kings and Lord of Lords, above all powers and Kingdoms is seeking YOU as a servant/soldier in His blessed army. You can make a difference!

The choice is ours. That means each one of us needs to immediately RETURN to our nation's spiritual foundation, God, and REPENT. This is the case regardless of how highly we may perceive our own level of righteousness with God. It is critical that EVERY person audibly confess that they have sinned both individually and as a member of our nation.

> Who can say, I have made my heart clean, I am pure from my sin? *Proverbs 20:9*

Each person needs to be the living embodiment of the act of repentance, turning away from evil if we desire to see the repentance of the masses in our country and world.

For ALL have sinned and fallen short of the glory of God. *Romans 3:23*

We need to continue repenting and praying each day until we see God's hand miraculously transform and restore our personal and national life.

If my people who are called by My name humble themselves, pray, seek My face, and turn from their wicked ways, then I will hear from heaven, will forgive their sin, and will heal their land. *Second Chronicles 7:14*

Conclusion

I committed to experiment with the ABC Challenge in the springtime of 2012 and completed it on June 17, Father's Day. It was late Sunday afternoon when I reached page 1,226, the last page in the book of Revelation. I stood up, laughed aloud and shouted, "Yes!" At that time, I had no way of knowing that this particular 2012 ABC process would inspire me to write this book called, Heaven Rules, during the next 60 days. I might have shouted louder if I had known what was about to happen as a direct result of accessing the KEY by ABC!

When I closed the Bible that afternoon, I felt like I had just finished hiking the 2,167-mile Appalachian Trail.[29] This wilderness trail spans a distance from Georgia in the south to Maine in the north. It consists of narrow, winding footpaths meandering along the highest ridges and through the valleys below throughout the continuous steep mountain ranges. It takes approximately 6 months to complete that exhausting, challenging hiking course. Every year, thousands of adventure seeking hikers

29

commit to walking the Appalachian Trail in the spring. Interestingly, only three people in twenty actually finish the course.

If I successfully hiked the Appalachian Trail, I can imagine myself standing triumphantly atop the tallest peak with skinned knees and bloody knuckles! Tremendous satisfaction must fill the one who reaches that goal. The brave hiker must be exhilarated standing there breathing in the fresh mountain air! I felt a similar sense of accomplishment, a rush, when I came to the last page of the ABC challenge. I also felt somewhat bruised and battered because completing the ABC was definitely a challenge!

You start by opening the Bible to Genesis 1:1. You will begin with the first line, reading one page at a time, amounting to 12-14 pages each day. There will be unfamiliar words and phrases and you will not understand all of what you read. That will not stop you. It is a race against time limits! You are under pressure, and a prize of eternal value awaits you if you are tough enough to make it to the finish line! The devil will fight you and cause distractions to keep you from completing the task. You must resist him and finish at all costs.

"I press on to reach the end of the race and receive the heavenly prize for which God, through Christ Jesus, is calling us." *Philippians 3:14*

It took me several weeks to get through the Old Testament. When I reached the New Testament, I was hungry for the Words of Jesus! The New Testament was as refreshing to me as cool water is to one dying of thirst. Certain elation filled me up when I reached that wonderful Holy text filled with Words of HOPE in the New Testament! I reached the finish line with an unmistakable sense of joy! I was completely delighted because once again, I found myself in that rare place of God's favor.

ABC will position me in that extraordinary place each time I engage in the process and there is no limit to how many times I engage in the process. I knew my deliberate act pleased God and that knowledge pleased me immensely. I felt like a five year old on Christmas Eve, filled with expectation and excitement! I found it difficult to contain my emotions, knowing God was smiling because of my action and accomplishment. I know if you complete the ABC, He will smile on you, too!

I also knew my act of completing the ABC process might affect others as well as myself. Your completion of the ABC process will have eternal implications for you and possible others as well! The ABC process is your opportunity to make a difference that "neither moth nor rust destroys, and thieves do not steal." (Matthew 6:20) This difference will manifest in your own life and in the lives of others in ways you cannot even imagine. Are you curious about the marvelous outcome that awaits you? Only you can make the decision to "commit and stay the course"! You will be glad you did! It is as simple as ABC. You will be PLAYING FOR KEEPS by HEAVEN RULES since it is indeed HEAVEN THAT RULES!

> The Lord preserves the faithful, and fully recompenses the proud doer. Be strong and let your heart take courage, all you who hope in the Lord. *Psalms 31:23, 24*

Notes

1. Mark Twain, This text is an excerpt from a letter written by Mark Twain to Olivia Langdon on 9/18/1869. Mark Twain Quotes (www.twainquotes.com).

2. Billy Graham, *Hope for the Troubled Heart*, p 53, Bantam Books, New York. Used by permission.

3. This information about Ted Cooper, Jr. was obtained from zondervan.com/coopert. Cooper found salvation in 1999 and established his ministry in 2002

4. This information about Ted Cooper, Jr. was obtained from zondervan.com/coopert.

5. Murray Gell-Mann. *The Quark and the Jaguar*, pp.264-265, Google books @ http://www.google.com/search?q=%22each+found+a+contradiction%22+Gell-Mann.

6. This information regarding the number of words in the Bible was an excerpt from wiki.answers.com.

7. www.answers.com. Metal compass information.

8. Hep.ucsb.edu/courses/ph23/chap19Text.pdf. *First Law of Thermodynamics*, chapter 18

9. Oswald Chambers, *My Utmost for His Highest*, Discovery House Publishers, Grand Rapids, MI 49501 Used by permission.

10. Janet Rumpf, author of *The Healing Brush*, submitted by author's second cousin, Peggy Culbert of Sewell, NJ . Janet Rumpf, *The Healing Brush*, Written permission obtained from surviving spouse, Dennis Desjardin, Richmond, Rhode Island.

11. Oswald Chambers, *My Utmost for His Highest*, Discovery House Publishers, Grand Rapids, MI 49501 Used by permission.

12. Oswald Chambers, *My Utmost for His Highest*, Discovery House Publishers, Grand Rapids, MI. 49501. Used by permission.

13. L. B. Cowman, *Streams in the Desert*, p 280, Zondervan Publishers, Grand Rapids, MI 49530. Used by permission.

14. L. B. Cowman, *Streams in the Desert*, p 222, Zondervan Publishers, Grand Rapids, MI 49530. Used by permission.

15. L. B. Cowman, *Streams in the Desert*, p 138, Zondervan Publishers, Grand Rapids, MI 49530 Used by permission.

16. Faye Aldridge, *Real Messages from Heaven*, 79, Destiny Image Publishers, Shippensburg, PA 2011 Used by permission.

17. Faye Aldridge, *Real Messages from Heaven*, 59, Destiny Image Publishers, Shippensburg, PA 2011 Used by permission.

18. Don Piper and Cecil Murphey, *Ninety Minutes in Heaven*, p 25, Revell a division of Baker Publishing 2004, Grand Rapids, MI 49516. Used by permission.

19. Robert Kastenbaum, *Is There Life After Death?* (New York: Prentice Hall, 1984) 25, citing G. A. Garfield in Kastenbaum, ed., *Between Life And Death* (New York: Spring Publishers, 1979), 54-55. Used by permission.

20. Marvin Ford, *On The Other Side*, citing George Godkin, (Plainfield: Logos International, 1978) 93-94. Used by permission.

21. Marietta Davis, Dennis and Nolene Prince, *Nine Days In Heaven*, p 73 (Charisma House, Lake Mary, FL 32746) 2011 Used by permission.

22. Marietta Davis, Dennis and Nolene Prince, *Nine Days In Heaven*, p 42-54 (Charisma House, Lake Mary, FL 32746) 2011 Used by permission.

23. Marietta Davis, Dennis and Nolene Prince, *Nine Days In Heaven*, P 73 Charisma House, Lake Mary, FL 32746) 2011 Used by permission.

24. Maurice Rawlings, *M.D. To Hell And Back* (Nashville, TN: Thomas Nelson Publishers, 1993) 91 Used by permission.

25. www.into thyword.org

26. www.vitalChristian.org

27. www.vitalChristian.org

28. Peggy Culbert, Sewell, New Jersey 08080

29. Statistics for the Appalachian Trail recorded from www.trailsource.comappalachian-trail/index.asp

Personal Notes

Other books by Faye Aldridge

A Fax From Heaven

A Fax From Heaven-Condensed Version

Real Messages From Heaven

Real Messages From Heaven -Volume 2

20342284R00087

Made in the USA
Charleston, SC
08 July 2013